LIVING IN
HELL

LIVING IN
HELL

The dilemma of African-American survival

MOSE PLEASURE, JR.
& FRED C. LOFTON
Editors

ZondervanPublishingHouse
Grand Rapids, Michigan

A Division of HarperCollinsPublishers

Living in Hell
Copyright © 1995 by Mose Pleasure, Jr., and Fred C. Lofton

Requests for information should be addressed to:

 ZondervanPublishingHouse
Grand Rapids, Michigan 49530

Library of Congress Cataloging-in-Publication Data

Living in hell: the dilemma of African-American survival / edited by Mose
    Pleasure, Jr., and Fred C. Lofton.
     p. cm.
    "A project of the Melas Ekklesia Group."
    Includes bibliographical references (p.).
    ISBN: 0-310-49781-7 (softcover)
    1. Sermons, American—Afro-American authors.   2. Afro-Americans—
Religion—Sermons.   3. United States—Moral conditions—Sermons.
I. Pleasure, Mose. II. Lofton, Fred C. III. Melas Ekkesia Group.
BV4241.5.L58 1995
252'.0089'96073—dc 20   95-12479
                                                             CIP

Edited by Victoria L. Johnson
Interior design by Sherri L. Hoffman

Printed in the United States of America

---

95 96 97 98 99 00 /❖DH/ 10 9 8 7 6 5 4 3 2

Contents

Sermons From the Old Testament

Sermons From the New Testament

Essays

Foreword

THE MELAS EKKLESIA GROUP

The Melas Ekklesia Group is a consortium of African-American ministers dedicated to developing, establishing, and maintaining social justice in America. The Greek words *melas ekklesia* mean "black church." The group emphasizes generating self-help in the African-American church and community, seeking to achieve empowerment for individual persons, and increasing stability and strength for African-American institutions and groups.

The Melas Ekklesia Group engages in activities which create and build links between the African-American church and community. They develop economic endeavors and strategies for use by the churches and community; enlist and encourage support for private and public agendas which enhance the creation and maintenance of linkages; develop and foster widespread understanding of the challenges to African-American existence; interpret the meaning and impact of American power within and upon the African-American church and community; commission and undertake research, analysis, and community education to eradicate the ills faced by the African-American community; and become the agent of last resort when it is necessary to achieve results hindered by normal channels of opportunity.

The Melas Ekklesia Group considers itself to be a place where African-American success can be experienced through the collaboration of excellence, ability, talent, and strength to revitalize the spirit and lift the horizons of the African-America church and community.

Preface

I was born black in the United States of America, as were the other contributors to this book. No matter what I accomplish or achieve, my existence as an African-American male (an entity thoroughly denigrated by American society as an excuse for enslavement and continued degradation) is always brought forth as the major fact for final arbitration as to my worth as a person. I am created by the Most High and am a child of God. However, America refuses to let me be who I am and constantly reminds me that I am not who I think I am.

I once heard the great preacher Dr. Howard Thurman say that the Romans would never allow Jesus to forget that he was a Jew under subjection to Rome. If a Roman wanted to kick him into the ditch, Jesus had no recourse. My experience in life is similar. In my hometown, African-American people were constantly put down by garbage-truck drivers (garbage workers who loaded the trash were black); postmen; landlords; and, of course, policemen and sheriff's deputies. White boys and girls made fun of us as they went by in buses, while we walked past their school on the way to ours (some of these same people did not believe in busing later on). White women made us go to the back door to ask for a job raking leaves.

When I attended Morehouse College in Atlanta, the famed Southern megalopolis where African-American people have achieved more than in most places in the South—even there I was suffused by a destructive, suffocating assault on my being.

Somewhere along the journey from slavery to freedom, the American system developed a trigger mechanism, a negative sensitivity to my African-American male presence. It became a technique designed to destroy anything empowering my existence as a man or recognizing my humanity. The trigger mechanism lay hidden away in the secret places of the white American psyche until it evolved into a politically palatable (politically correct!) statement of rejection of African-American people, which finally surfaced for general usage as America's (un)official domestic policy of *benign neglect*.

Both black and white persons tell me that these thoughts are merely painful memories from my past. What once was is no more. They believe that presidential decrees, current statistics, and laws disallow this trigger mechanism in a civilized society. I agree. And I disagree. Herein lies the dilemma of my personal African-American existence.

I knew a girl whose mother whipped her so much that she instinctively drew herself into a passively defensive posture each time her mother raised her hand. Once an individual is trained to live with personal assault as a fact of life, that person automatically responds within the prescribed mold.

Even in what is claimed to be *post-racist* America, I am unable to break the mold and loose the shackles. When I am alone in an elevator with a white woman, I am uncomfortably aware she can yell "rape" and bring my life, with all the achievements and honors precious to me, to an emasculating conclusion. Sometimes, as I sit in places of decision making and recognition in the wider Memphis community, I get the uneasy feeling I've been appointed to membership in the nucleus of those who will make the anti-black trigger mechanism work against coming generations of African-American men and women.

I'm an African-American who bought the old saw of connection between opportunity and hard work; achievement and aspiration; and moral rectitude and success. Today, I see none of these working for the great majority of those who are the products of benign neglect, and their stark existence grows worse instead of better.

If living in America is hell for me, an African-American man possessing a few of the trappings of success, then there can be no doubt concerning the pressures experienced by the majority of African-Americans existing at the bottom of the American ladder of success. This defines the burden of blackness in our time. Here's the truth of the matter: For African-American men and women, living in America is like living in hell.

This book of sermons and essays examines the reality of a people caught in the middle of a conflict between the American facts of life and God's promises enshrined and disclosed in Judeo-Christian tradition. Ministers, churches, and Americans of all sorts and persuasions will benefit from this multifaceted treatment of the plight of African-American people. Most of all, it is my hope that this book will help African-American men and women replace the rebellion and rage which living in hell inspires with the hope and assistance toward achievement which God grants in spite of it.

FRED C. LOFTON, PRESIDENT
THE MELAS EKKLESIA GROUP

Part I

SERMONS

From the

OLD

TESTAMENT

Go Get Lot

Genesis 13:11

Kevin Brian Willis, Sr. (B.A., Bishop College; further study, Perkins Theological Seminary, M.Div. program) is pastor of the Riverside Missionary Baptist Church of Memphis, Tennessee.

Go Get Lot

So Lot chose for himself all the Jordan Valley, and Lot journeyed east; thus they separated from each other (GENESIS 13:11 RSV).

Genetically, Lot was the son of Haran, grandson of Terah, and nephew of Abraham the patriarch. When Abram left Ur of the Chaldees, his hometown, and followed God's leading to a land promised to his descendants, his caravan included Lot, his nephew. Lot earned a notorious reputation because he separated from Abram and "moved his tents as far as Sodom" (Genesis 13:12). He not only lived in Sodom, but also became a participating citizen of that community.

Lot's tragedy had nothing to do with what he owned. Abram possessed more material goods than his nephew. Lot made poor choices. He became a captive, not of what he owned, but of what possessed him. A pleasure-seeking lifestyle and the absence of personal values led to a downward road to hell and destructive consequences.

What began as a noble quest of faith in Ur of the Chaldees became a sinful pursuit driven by lust in Sodom. Lot did not represent God, nor did his presence exert any saving power on the people in Sodom. He became merely one additional member of Sodomite society and culture, a representative of human degradation at its very worst.

1. Who Is Lot?

The Lot of Hebrew history represents a *type* of man. This kind of person closely resembles a current generation of African-American men, rich in heritage and culture but held captive. They are trapped and bound by the pursuit of immediate prosperity. Their militant mentality uses illiteracy, unemployment, and poverty as excuses for irresponsibility, decadence, and a tendency toward living at the bottom rung of life. Modern-day Lots separate themselves from the power available in God, family, and institutions, which would make them capable of positively developing their dynamic manhood.

2. WHAT CAUSED LOT'S CAPTIVITY?

Lot became a prisoner through his identification with and citizenship in Sodom. His relationship with the people there caused him to become a victim of war for the Kings of the Shev. Several cities rebelled against paying tribute to King Ched-or-laomer. Lot participated in the war. This conflict did not glorify God or work in Lot's best interest. Consequently, Lot became a prisoner-of-war in a confrontation he did not initiate. Abram had to immediately organize and arm his servants to rescue his nephew from captivity.

Although the depth of Lot's sinfulness and depravity became evident when he chose to reside in Sodom, his troubles began in Egypt. Lot journeyed with Abram to Egypt when he temporarily left Canaan to escape the famine. Lot loved Egypt. So when Abram gave him a choice of land, Lot compared the plains of Jordan with what he had witnessed in the land of Egypt. Intoxicated with desire, Lot was powerfully drawn to the beautiful, lush, "well-watered" Jordan.

Lot craved a promise from God, equal to Abram's, along with prosperity and possessions. He sought to establish this through Sodomite citizenship, coupled with social, political, economic, and personal relationships with the people in the land.

Many young African-American men develop a materialistic mentality like Lot's. The Lot living in Sodom (Genesis 14) is not the same person adopted by his uncle Abram when they left Ur of the Chaldees (Genesis 12). The perversions of Egypt polluted his personality and destroyed his integrity.

Lot changed because Abram, Lot's mentor, changed. Lot watched Abram become a man who believed in the extreme importance of materialistic gain and wealth. Lot observed his uncle transform into a conspirator and a liar. Lot's environment and experience produced corrupt morals and standards. He acted out of his orientation and example. Remember, Lot's father, Haran, died and Abram became his "father figure." What Abram displayed in Egypt, Lot became in Sodom.

Perhaps the plight of contemporary Lots is the result of wrong examples. Maybe the model of an older generation of black men caused the decline of young African-American men today. Has the older generation of shiftless black men created a new generation of African-American men who become fathers without consideration for mother or child? Has the previous abusive husband discredited the institution of marriage in the minds of many, creating the sinful institution known as "common-law marriage?" Have the drunkards and winos of yesteryear evolved into the dopeheads and junkies of today? Maybe an aggressive, abusive society molded all of these possibilities.

Lot's trouble came because of his residence in Sodom. His captivity was the result of his love of the world and his desire to share its wicked perversions. Lot's captivity can be blamed on poor leadership by those commissioned and called to set the right example. Not only for Lot, but for the world.

3. WHY SHOULD LOT BE RESCUED?

Lot should be rescued because of his captivity. King Bera of Sodom and his allies fled from the advancing King Ched-or-laomer in the valley of the Shev. They left Lot unprotected. The enemy seized his family, servants, property, and livestock. Lot's possessions were about to be distributed among his captors. Lot faced the danger of losing his life. That is why Abram moved quickly to rescue him from any further deterioration of circumstances. If Abram had hesitated it might have caused Lot's death.

Similarly, modern-day Lot is captured by the supreme enemy, Satan. The adversary imbeds himself in the society, culture, and economy of America. Not only is contemporary Lot the prisoner of Satan, but his valuable, made-in-the-image-of-God existence is also seized. He is no longer able to think and reason for himself. His manhood, free will, and self-worth are all ensnared. He is in danger of being destroyed.

Satan places no value on a modern-day Lot's life. The enemy does not merely desire to enslave or hold him for ransom. He wants to kill him—spiritually, emotionally, physically, and mentally. Satan knows that any race of people can be annihilated if the men are wiped out.

Lot must be rescued because he is a member of the family. Abram says to Lot, "We are brethren" (Genesis 13:8 NKJV). Abram refers to their kinship in the same family. Abram made it clear when he used the term "brethren" that differences of opinion, separation by residence, or conflict need not have a negative effect on family relations. Abram expressed his responsibility for Lot; the family cannot progress while a member is captive.

Abram rescued Lot because Abram disobeyed the command of God concerning his nephew. When God called Abram, he told him, "Get thee out of thy country, and from thy kindred, and from thy father's house" (Genesis 12:1 KJV). God made him "the Father of a New Nation." Father Abraham became responsible for the generation of his day and for all the ensuing generations.

Lot has to be released because he made a mistake, and mistakes are not terminal with God. Lot's life is riddled with bad choices. First, he "lifted up his eyes and beheld" the seduction of materialism. Second, he greedily chose for himself "all the plain of the Jordan" (Genesis 13:11 NKJV). Third, he "separated" himself from his "father," Abram. Fourth, he dwelt in the cities of the plain. Fifth, he "pitched his tent toward Sodom." And sixth, he made Sodom his home.

Lot's trouble came because of wrong choices. However, Lot's rescue cannot be postponed or abandoned based on his errors. If mistakes are the reason for not reaching out to the lost captives, none of us would be alive!

"All have sinned and fall short." The redeeming grace and mercy of God did not abandon us because of our shortcomings. Nor does God destroy people for their mistakes. Like the loving father in the Parable of the Prodigal Son, he did not scold or chide his son, but joyfully welcomed him back into the family. God's understanding and love is waiting. He desires that all of his prodigal sons come to themselves and return to him.

Likewise, the church cannot ignore the plight of African-American brothers because of wrong choices they may have made. How to make right decisions cannot be taught by ignoring these brothers. Moreover, if Christians fail to rescue a Lot among us, then we are guilty of making a wrong choice. Lot's life is valuable. The church can't afford to let Lot be obliterated because we disagree with how he thinks, where he lives, and the people he chooses to associate with.

Christians should not condone Lot's behavior, but neither can we leave him to die. Surely, Abram did not want to separate from Lot. Abram wanted solidarity of outlook and outcome within his family, but Lot made other choices. Instead of Abram trying to force his convictions on Lot, he allowed his nephew the opportunity to make his own decisions. The church must follow Abram's example. Rescuing Lot will place him educationally, socially, and of course, spiritually, in a position where he can make positive choices, before it's too late. Lot is a member of the family. Christians must support and love Lot, even when he makes disappointing choices that result in devastating consequences for himself and the community.

4. How Can We Rescue Lot?

Abram heard about Lot's captivity. "And when Abram heard that his relative had been taken captive, he led out his trained men, born in his house, three hundred and eighteen, and went in pursuit as far as Dan" (Genesis 14:14 NASB). Abram did not employ all of his servants in Lot's rescue. "Trained servants" is the first prerequisite for those chosen. The church of Christ is the only agency qualified to rescue Lot. Its trained servants are empowered by the Holy Spirit. They know the biblical foundations of the execution and art of rescue. The Christian ministry is developed and designed exclusively for Lot. Churches are trained and specialize in recovery missions. The church's methods of rescue are:

1. Preaching
2. Teaching
3. Evangelism
4. Love and Patience

The church is trained for recovery missions, but is also armed for battle. The second prerequisite for releasing contemporary Lot is "armed servants." The church of God possesses spiritual weapons: the powerful Word of God which reproves, rebukes, and exhorts; the Holy Spirit; and a consuming compassion to set at liberty those held captive.

The last criterion for the identity of rescuers is that they are "servants born out of the house of Abram." This refers to trained, armed servants, but also to those recruited especially for their ability to make the journey. They are capable of withstanding the wear and tear associated with a long, tedious battle.

There are some who suggest Lot ought to be left to die, because any effort to rescue him is too expensive for one so undeserving. Some believe captivity and death are just rewards for modern-day Lots who align themselves with the wickedness of the current Sodom. Not so! The body of Christ must be motivated by love and understanding concerning Lot's predicament.

Like Abram, it is essential for the church to be Lot's kinsman-deliverer and to move with urgency to free Lot and restore his integrity. In order to accomplish this, the church must go where Lot dwells. Jesus, in the "Parable of the Great Feast," commands the church to "Go get Lot." At suppertime the Master says to the servant, "Go out quickly into the streets and lanes of the city, . . . and bring in hither the poor, and the maimed, and the halt, and the blind" (Luke 14:23, 21 KJV). Jesus said, "Go where Lot is, and deal with who Lot is."

Lot *may not be able* to come to us because he's a hungry, homeless man living in a cardboard hut under the freeway, an inmate in a state or federal prison, addicted to and held captive by drugs, or a resident in the city prison called the "projects." If the church feels compassion for Lot and desires to restore him, we've got to go get him. That means moving outside of the arrogance of education and occupation and leaving the comfort and security of our homes and sanctuaries. We've got to go get Lot, because Lot desperately needs our help. ✢

Living in Hell:
America the Unprincipled Place

Genesis 39:7–9

David A. Hall (B.A., Butler University; M.Div.,
Interdenominational Theological Center; D.Min.,
McCormick Theological Seminary) is pastor of the
Temple Church of God in Christ in Memphis,
Tennessee.

David A. Hall

Living in Hell: America the Unprincipled Place

And it came to pass after these things, that his master's wife cast her eyes upon Joseph; and she said, Lie with me. But he refused, and said unto his master's wife, Behold, my master wotteth not what is with me in the house, and he hath committed all that he hath to my hand; there is none greater in this house than I; neither hath he kept back any thing from me but thee, because thou art his wife: how then can I do this great wickedness, and sin against God? (GENESIS 39:7–9 KJV).

To refer to America as an unprincipled place is paradoxical. Due to the broad respect this nation receives for being the champion of guaranteed human dignity, equality, and rights, it is hard to imagine this country as immoral.

Many revere America for her invincible "can do" spirit and her inherent standards of fair play, moral customs, and practice of law. The United States stands virtually alone as the most imitated nation on earth. American culture is everywhere.

America also reveres freedom of religion. Here people can practice the tenets of any faith without persecution or prohibition. Certainly, any country receiving such high honor should be one of the few places on earth where religious practices and social conventions coexist without strain or conflict.

On the contrary, real tensions do exist in America. Pointless battles occur between conventions of law and social custom, morality and politics, and faith and culture. In America the once compatible, supportive moral standards and the practices of society have now separated, due to the challenging dynamism of situational and existential philosophies.

Furthermore, basic to her character flaw is America's inability to live up to her high founding principles. America is quickly losing the liberties for which she stands. This is no longer "one nation under God, indivisible"—if in fact it ever was.

How does the reality of America's unprincipled existence become seen for what it is? Sociologists espouse one theory: Stress occurs in the minority elements of the society and provides initial warning about significant problems endemic to the general society. Historically, the founding creeds of America have been subjugated to the power elite, race prejudice, and wealth.

Today in America, the truth which made her great is diminished. This country, often likened to heaven on earth, has become a living hell for African-Americans. Make no mistake, the practical essence of hell is being actualized today in the physical realities of African-American people.

Particularly threatened are the poorly educated, self-defeated, frustrated African-American men between eighteen and thirty-five years of age. America's hell for them is an unfruitful compromise without hope. This hell dares them to achieve and at the same time annihilates them for cutting against the grain. America systematically denies African-American people success. They experience a double standard, unprincipled circumstances of social injustice, and biased politics. America is where "guaranteed" freedoms and opportunities are voided daily for people of color and for the underprivileged.

Ultimately, one realizes the American way is creating wholesale confusion within the ranks of the disappointed and despondent. The only principle African-American men recognize is one of constant illusion, wherein the American dream is a cruel hoax. Ironically, the principles of America have been patronized, politicized, and polarized by the well-meaning advocates of social justice and bigotry alike. America's unprincipled character is a systemic malady and not a sickness ascribed to any one individual or race. The entire nation is affected by this unethical existence. As a result, it teeters near the edge of moral and systemic bankruptcy.

In the Church of God in Christ, men are raised to believe first in God and secondly in the value of a good education. It is understood that a faithful heart and a prepared mind will take a person through every obstacle. This is the classic irony. Even in the face of America's diminished educational system, Pentecostals persistently believe that being prepared will make the difference between failure and success.

Lately, the teaching and learning processes have been challenged by the ills of society. Hopeful projections about this country's future are made by religious leaders, educators, and especially, the conservative right. A persistently growing illusion exists: unprincipled America is becoming greater, in spite of this country's lessening commitment to the welfare, education, and equality of all people. America is the land of opportunity, but if an educated African-American should make it, he could become a freak to his own people, a showpiece in the larger society, or a workhorse for the system.

In America, nobody is who they appear to be. Consider the following example and how this relates to the vulnerable position in which African-Americans are placed: America can be compared to an individual standing in front of a mirror. The person views his entire body in the mirror from head to toe. The reflected image informs the individual of what they truly are, right? Wrong! The replica in the mirror does not tell the whole story about the individual. The reproduction in the mirror is flat, lacking the person's true personality and perspective.

America appears to treat all people in this country the same way, like the image reflected in the mirror appears to tell about the individual standing before it. One naturally assumes the message from the reflection is always true, but is it? The picture in the mirror does not tell the whole story.

How does the person in the mirror discover the truth? How do African-American men deal with the mirror game they are forced to play? One way to test the truth of a mirror's reflection is to write something on a sheet of paper and hold it before the mirror: the message comes back unintelligible. At this point the established illusion is exposed as ingenious manipulation. America tries to suggest that everything for all people in this country is the same. However, the individual in the mirror must turn the message around or read it backwards in order to get a true understanding. For African-American men, the message reflected by society must likewise be constantly turned around.

In other words, after getting a fix on the American illusion, one comes to understand that African-Americans must keep turning the message around. America's character always has been and shall remain unprincipled, convoluted, and unredeemable at heart. In order to authenticate the reflection from the American mirror, African-Americans must accept the violation of society's promised conventions. Then, at the same time they must appeal to the unprincipled and oppressive system for legitimate privileges and rights. Only when the message is turned around can African-Americans truly understand that the mirror of American principle and opportunity is an illusion. This is the demeaning, confusing, and dishonorable American way. Make no mistake about the surreal qualities of American bigotry: they are reflected in every message. As a consequence, ignorance and innocence are fleeting experiences, a real detriment to African-American men who learn too slowly.

African-Americans understand the illusion behind the slogan "America, Love It or Leave It!" African-Americans regard this country as home; therefore, we must and do love it. To leave it is out of the question. Alex Haley helped African-Americans to bridge the time gap slavery created. African-Americans understand how much dignity and power have been systematically denied them due to inequality of opportunity, restricted privileges, unlawful justice, and racial bias. America's constant failures truly hurt and damage those who believe the strongest in its values.

As a result of not having the power to control the African-American life agenda, black men rebel. Consequently, disproportionate numbers of African-American men are incarcerated; many turn homosexual, become abusive husbands, desert their families, or simply give up on life. Possibly worse is the sight of an African-American man living the unprincipled American illusion himself. He believes that selling out his character, training, customs, and even his race in order to *get ahead in life* is okay.

African-American men have little hope. The years of bitter struggle profoundly affect them. The Negro National Anthem by James Weldon Johnson, "Lift Every Voice and Sing," speaks directly to the tragedy of constant loss. The second stanza says, "Stony the road we trod, bitter the chastening rod, felt in the days when hope, unborn, had died."[1]

For African-American men, hope always dies unborn. Yet, the vast majority blindly believe in the unprincipled hell of America's illusion, until it becomes too much to deal with. They believe their home and religious training will carry them through, even after they discover, analyze, and engage the fallacy.

If America would only live up to her principles! Alas, the realities of the broken underpinnings and axioms of this society make the reflection of America too distorted to believe in or deal with. Too often the African-American reads the message contained in the American illusion and sadly replies, "Change may come, but not in my lifetime." Honestly, this is enough to make one smash the mirror.

In America, where faith is significant and dynamic, many African-American men disassociate themselves from their religious roots. An ominous reality on the horizon says that a large percentage of African-American men have totally given up on organized religion. Abuse of drugs, sex, and other forms of escapism have become the overriding method for dealing with the hell in America. At one time, the major sources of coping with America's racial challenges included the principles of religion and a good strict home training. The African-American church used to be the center of financial, personal, and institutional control. The torment in America that black males are experiencing today creates departure from the ranks of the church.

These same circumstances are causing our own unprincipled departure from the preaching, teaching, and belief in a disciplining, powerful Gospel. The lack of religious standards builds the foundation for excuses and perpetuation of moral and spiritual weakness among generations of African-American men.

All African-American men must exist within the realities of America. They live with the double standards, racial prejudice, gross unemployment, and skillfully organized attempts to frustrate their every effort. Caucasian-American culture views the problems within the African-American community as a ruse for promoting fear, rationale for resentment, and also retaliation against the victims of demonic and systematic oppression by white America.

Is there any wonder some African-Americans are out of touch with the empowerment of religion, business, and self-reliance? They lack a proper response to the struggle and compensate with superficial characteristics which set a distinguishing tone of difference between blacks and whites; the haves and have-nots. There are four basic types of African-American men emerging from the struggle with America's unprincipled fallacy. I refer to the first type of African-American man as the *This Is Me!* character. For instance, nobody can "cool walk" like this type of brother. The dominant culture cannot deal with this man's dynamic, strange, and often unintelligible patterns of slang. His latest hairdo always sends a counter-culture message. This man's sense of vanity and pride is evident, even when he is dead wrong. This is the kind of brother who "pimp-walks" before the camera while appearing on the six o'clock news for robbing a candy store with a toy pistol and netting fifty dollars. These characteristics represent his only dignity. They carry little weight beyond a show of defiance. To his dying day he will shout, "This is me whether you like it or not!"

It is impossible for the second type of African-American man to make a bold stand like the *This is Me* brother. He exists within the realm of raw, sheer dilemma. I refer to him as the *Trade-Off Man*. It can be overwhelming for him to face the unprincipled monster alone. The situation in America offers a twisted delusion which fosters the trade-off of black hopes, values, and personality; this seems both necessary and acceptable. The hell of America causes this second type of African-American man to forget the first law of nature, socially speaking, which is "to protect one's self at all times." *Trade-Off Men* lay down their humanity and values, giving the system the essence of their character merely to "make it in America." This character used to be known as "Uncle Tom." Now he appears on the scene as the discredited politician, a ne'er-do-well and opportunist who deals without principle. He is a self-serving glutton after the order of Jacob's brother, Esau, in the Old Testament.

Trading off has not always been a matter of selfish choice. Strangely, there is a subgrouping of *Trade-Off Men* who are victims. This man portrays a human face and dignity. He labors in order to survive. Historically, African-American men survived by whatever means necessary. This point needs to be understood. The haunting specter of Georgia Douglas Johnson's poem *Old Black Men* presents a classic example of the mixture of resignation and hope in African-American men who are forced to submit, are beaten down and struggling. Their resignation is society's shame, a bitter root deep in the soil of the American experience. They have no more of themselves to give. This group traded life's frustration and failure for personal sanity.

> They have dreamed as young men dream
> Of glory, love and power;
> They have hoped as youth will hope
> Of life's sun-minted hour.
> They have seen as others saw

Their bubbles burst in air,
And they have learned to live it down
As though they did not care.[2]

I refer to the third group of black men as the *Have-It-Mades*. They are not beaten down to nothing while attempting to stand and challenge America. In this society of very successful, high-profile individuals, a few African-Americans are determined to make it. They have decided to play the game by the rules of the illusion, bearing in mind that their strength is in manipulating the system and bending the rules. These are the few who stand at the mirror, realizing the message is twisted, yet saying with confidence, "I am going to make it." This group includes the very talented, physically gifted, intellectual, and connected persons of the African-American community.

Many of them "make it to the big time!" Some of them accomplish this and manage to remain black. African-Americans will continue to applaud their superstars while at the same time cautioning them to keep looking back and extending a helping hand. They should never forget "from whence they came." Of course, their challenge is to survive success, leaving footprints and a trail for coming generations to follow.

The fourth type of African-American man who is emerging from the struggle is the principled individual called the *Regular Fellas*. He is not a beaten-down man, though he is challenged and wounded daily. Neither has he decided to trade himself off for a taste of success. His only connection is his innate drive to achieve, his self-reliance, and his values. He will never be rich, but he is committed to educating his children. He and his brothers are the glue, the very "stuff" helping African-American communities stand strong under the threat of hopeless behavior caused by economic deprivation. They endure and will make it, for their own sakes. For them, making it in America does not mean measuring up to the dominant culture's standard or separation from their own values. They walk the stable ground of "work a day, make a day." They are not bitter; neither are they satisfied with their standard of living or potential for a brighter future.

For each type of African-American man, one abiding question remains, "What does it take to make it in America?" Of course, the answer manifests itself in various ways, but the heartbeat of aspiration remains the same, "Lord, I want to make it!"

Some African-Americans believe that to exist in America it is necessary to engage in a tragic love affair with an unprincipled partner—for example, military service. America is simply saying to youth, "The United States of America will accept your bodies as collateral for your future advancement." Fighting and dying in combat had become a necessary risk for advancement for African-American youth (the Persian Gulf War was one example), even when one is taught against such activity. I'm convinced war and politics of war are a delight to some Western men. They know how to kill! No one kills any better than white European males. But there are ample groups of polarized people of color to do the killing for them. The unprincipled influence of America upon religious people must be counteracted before the state applies enough pressure to usurp God's position. Of course, this would be the ultimate posture of illusion.

In order for African-Americans to deal with the misconceptions in America, faith in God, a strong belief in one's self, and a solid moral base are very important. Joseph is a biblical example of one who faithfully endured trials while enslaved. Joseph's response to the circumstance in which Potiphar's wife placed him offers a model of self-denial and ethical security. Joseph's story is a useful guide for today's African-American man in similar circumstances. Joseph teaches self-control and self-respect through his experience. Note the similarities between Joseph's experience and that of African-American men:

Like black men, Joseph was sold into slavery by his brothers
Like black men, he was carried to a strange and distant land
Like black men, he was resold and given work beneath his
    dignity to do

Like black men, Joseph excelled at whatever he was given to
do because he tried harder
Like black men, the more he did better, the more was put on
him
Like black men, he became a matter of fascination to his
slave holder and a sex object to his slaveholder's woman
Like black men, he was left unprotected and responsible to
answer rumors, lies, and sick games played constantly to
bring him down

Joseph suffered misfortune not on the basis of trickery and
deceit, but because he held fast to his honor and self-respect. As
a slave, Joseph (like the African-American man) never forgot he
possessed dignity. The Scriptures explain Joseph's dilemma, "And
it came to pass after these things, that his master's wife cast her
eyes upon Joseph and said, 'Lie with me.' But he refused, and
said unto his master's wife, 'Behold, my master wotteth not what
is with me in the house, and he hath committed all that he hath
to my hand; There is none greater in this house than I; neither
hath he kept back any thing from me but thee, because thou art
his wife: how then can I do this great wickedness, and sin against
God?'" (Genesis 39:7–9).

The challenge for African-American men today is not sleeping with Potiphar's wife. She is just the symbol of the illusion.
One of the African-American man's main problems is escaping
her while struggling to manipulate a way through present-day
Egypt. African-Americans must be like Joseph; he never lost his
integrity. He always kept his head on straight and never forgot
the hell of slavery. African-American men must never lose sight
of the fact we may yet be slaves, even after owning businesses,
making agendas, controlling households, and powerfully cor-
recting unfair, unequal circumstances. Sleeping with Potiphar's
wife will not make us equal, nor provide an open door to freedom. Gratification is a momentary and fleeting emotion. Sexual
interludes will only lead to greater entanglement and bitter reality brought about due to a lack of discipline. Power is never given

or found through unprincipled activities, but only through the legitimate circumstance of self-reliance, self-respect, and the ability to absorb both good and bad with stability. Character alone can help African-Americans deal with the unprincipled American illusion.

It is time to stand up against the violations of humanity and dignity. The pain of black people is not incomprehensible, but it is a shame and blight on the conscience of America. If America cannot understand, then African-Americans must help her understand. People of color must program themselves away from the self-destruction, division, and anger which lead to constant embarrassment and continued victimization. It is necessary to interpret the events of the past and present in order to lead us to success in the future. Success must come without detrimental compromise, censorship, or delay, which by any other name is capitulation to a destructive system.

I hear the words of Paul, "For we wrestle not against flesh and blood, but against principalities, against powers, against the rulers of the darkness of this world, against spiritual wickedness in high places" (Ephesians 6:12). Paul's experiences included association with jailers, wicked people, and hardship, yet he states, "Brethren, I count not myself to have apprehended: but this one thing I do, forgetting those things which are behind, and reaching forth unto those things which are before, I press toward the mark for the prize of the high calling of God in Christ Jesus" (Philippians 3:13–14).

In conclusion, physical realities and obstacles *can* be overcome by faith. Jesus will not stand for his disciples to misread, misunderstand, or to live in a world of illusion. Remember the man healed of blindness? (Mark 8:22–26).

After being healed he saw the world through an illusionary perception. The confused man said, "I see men as trees, walking." Jesus had to touch him again (Mark 8:24–25).

The illusion of a principled America is being exposed daily by those to whom changing America is critical. African-American people have no argument with individual white brothers and sisters. They too are fighting this unprincipled illusion monster. "We wrestle not against flesh and blood, but against powers and spiritual wickedness in high places."

Hell in the right context is judgment upon those rendered powerless against sin. No praying people will forever struggle in hell. The Lord will not forsake his children. It is his will to deliver them. We must trust him to lead us through this hell. ✞

Notes

1. Quoted in Langston Hughes and Arna Bontemps, *The Poetry of the Negro* (New York: Doubleday Anchor, 1970), 32.

2. Ibid., 72.

From Heaven to Hell: What Went Wrong in Egypt?

Exodus 1:6–14

Alan V. Ragland (B.A., University of Memphis; M.Div., Colgate Rochester Divinity School; D.Min., McCormick Theological Seminary) is pastor of the Third Baptist Church in Chicago, Illinois.

From Heaven to Hell: What Went Wrong in Egypt?

And Joseph died, and all his brethren, and all that generation. And the children of Israel were fruitful, and increased abundantly, and multiplied, and waxed exceeding mighty; and the land was filled with them. Now there arose up a new king over Egypt, which knew not Joseph. And he said unto his people, Behold, the people of the children of Israel are more and mightier than we: Come on, let us deal wisely with them; lest they multiply, and it come to pass, that, when there falleth out any war, they join also unto our enemies, and fight against us, and so get them up out of the land. Therefore they did set over them taskmasters to afflict them with their burdens. And they built for Pharaoh treasure cities, Pithom and Raamses. But the more they afflicted them, the more they multiplied and grew. And they were grieved because of the children of Israel. And they made the children of Israel to serve with rigour: And they made their lives bitter with hard bondage, in mortar, and in brick, and in all manner of service in the field: all their service, wherein they made them serve, was with rigour (Exodus 1:6–14 KJV).

In this life, it is dangerous to interpret present affluent circumstances as enduring conditions. A hymn writer aptly reminds us, "Time is filled with swift transition." Changing times can create a variety of circumstances and conditions—a haven one day, a hell hole tomorrow. An oasis of promise may turn out to be a desert of distress.

These facts about transition are truthful realities evident in contemporary urban America. Families living in urban centers experience grief because of their choice not to flee the cities. Peaceful neighborhoods evolve into violent war zones of economic and social deterioration. Homes intended to be personal castles seem like prison cells. Dreams of life's endless possibilities are now merely protection against a growing and invading sense of death.

This kind of turbulence occurs in a society when the climate of social relationships changes: hospitality gives way to hostility; inclusiveness becomes intolerance; potential for prosperity in the society modifies from a broad opportunity to narrow competition; committed humanitarian leadership is replaced by selfish and self-serving political opportunists, seeking to be served rather than serving the citizen. One's status in society changes from that of a respected citizen to an economic utility, at best, and an economic liability, at worst.

The stunning, startling impact of this reality is that all of this can happen without the apparent victim doing anything, and there's the rub! In these swift social transitions, one might be tempted to assume that the recipient is merely a victim of unjust external influences. While this is a large portion of reality, it is not the whole truth. In most cases, we who consider ourselves victims are also benign accomplices to these evil transformations. In those ominous circumstances there seems to me to be a complex conspiracy of social ill will on the part of powerful oppressive forces and a self-indicting naivete on the part of those caught in this living hell. It is naivete which I want to examine so there is both a prophetic and a promising word for our troubled condition.

The dramatic event in the last chapters of Genesis is the unfolding destiny of Jacob and his descendants. These chapters outline their return from exile to the land of heritage and promise. The story is grounded in Jacob's covenant with God at Bethel (chapter 28 and reiterated in chapter 35). Jacob is designated an heir to God's promise to make Abraham and his descendants a great nation and give them the land of Canaan.

Joseph, the favored son of Jacob, experiences a series of unpredictable twists and troubling circumstances as the Old Testament drama unfolds. However, his eventual prosperity makes him the forerunner of God's provision for Jacob's family in Egypt during a difficult season of famine in Canaan. So the family's nomadic pilgrimage strangely leads them away from their sacred grounds in Canaan to seek economic relief in Egypt. The journey into Egypt occurs at Joseph's invitation and with God's permission, supposedly, for the next five years, until this economic storm passes (Genesis 45:6–11).

The writer of Genesis hints at how Jacob's family fared in Egypt. In the Egyptian province of Goshen, Jacob and his descendants prospered both in possessions and population. The Genesis account casually mentions Jacob's "seventeen-year" tenure in Egypt until his death. Before he died he requested to be buried in the promised land of Canaan. Already he seemed to have an ominous sense of the Israelites' temptation and dependence if they continued to live in Egypt.

Joseph and his brothers obeyed their father's deathbed wish and buried him Canaan. Then, Jacob's sons returned to live securely in Egypt for several generations, while Joseph continued to rule as Pharaoh's second in command. Joseph died at one hundred and ten years old. His final burial instructions, like Jacob's, found their roots in the memory of the land of his fathers. He envisioned the family eventually leaving Egypt, under God's direction.

After Joseph's death, Jacob's family continued to prosper in Egypt (Exodus 1:6–7). However, the winds of popularity and prosperity changed. A new Pharaoh emerged. A new ethnic conservatism invaded the political air. The extended economic privilege offered to the Israelites in Joseph's day became a political and economic threat. "There arose a Pharaoh who knew not Joseph," nor cared for the welfare of his descendants. The Hebrews became aliens, lost all previous privileges, and were made to become slaves of the new Egyptian order. The Israelites became that society's economically disenfranchised people. Their former prosperity was siphoned off to others and the Jewish nation was reduced to brutal poverty.

Unfortunately, blessings and curses often travel in close company. With every blessing we discover new dimensions of potential curses. This is a helpful lifetime lesson to learn. Evil hangs around good, looking for a devouring opportunity.

What happened in Egypt? What happened in America? The sinful side of humanity segregated these societies into social castes, fracturing the broad ethic of community and pitting the them(s) against the us(es); the haves against the have-nots. The minorities in America and the Israelites in Egypt both were reduced to non-persons as racism institutionalized.

The oppressed Hebrews often cried out with the undeniable truth, "The Egyptians did it to us." However, looking at the Israelites with an African-American eye of introspective social exegesis, ample evidence points to the agreeable and favorable participation on the part of the victims in developing their own hellish circumstances.

The first characteristic of this participation is complacency and comfort of prosperity. Nothing creates human inertia more than being satisfied with present conditions. The Israelites became stationary in the abundance of their Egyptian lifestyle. This attitude crossed subsequent generations, resulting in devastating effects on their sense of being a people of godly purpose.

Second, the Israelites voluntarily learned the Egyptian value system and bought into it uncritically for long stretches of time (that is, of course, until the rules changed when the new inferior values were involuntarily imposed). It's gravely dangerous for a people when their primary aspiration is merely to assimilate.

Third, the Israelites lived in Egypt unaccountable to anyone, for a lengthy duration, and lost their sense of timing. What started out as an interim survival strategy for five years turned into a 430-year residency. "They stayed where they were only supposed to stop over" (Walter Thomas, Progressive National Baptist Convention, 1989). Individuals set themselves up for obvious disappointment residing at God's rest stops.

Fourth, the Israelites lost the pilgrim instinct, forgetting their long-standing positions as sojourners and nomads, from Abraham through Jacob. Before coming to Egypt, God governed the people. They experienced the freedom to follow a divine lead. Israel's future success depended on how closely they followed God. But after settling in Egypt, they became geographical residents instead of wandering, searching, and trusting pilgrims. They came forth as social, spiritual, and eventually, economic domesticates.

Consequently, the Hebrew children developed a distorted sense of destination, preferring the present material prosperity and social comfort of Goshen to the future promise of Canaan, a land flowing with milk and honey.

African-Americans are well acquainted with how the quest for the holy city is often traded for the possession of the American dream. When "we have arrived" takes the place of "we're marching to Zion," we have lost the real sense that our ultimate destination is rooted in God.

Additionally, I am sure notions of individual prosperity among some of the Hebrews fractured the nation's unity. Wealth divided the ethnic sense of collective experience and common destiny. The Egyptians used the slave hierarchy to undermine the cohesiveness necessary for the nation to be liberated (for example, the middle-class Hebrew taskmasters). The early African-American freedom strategy from oppressive circumstances, introduced by W. E. B. Dubois, called the "talented tenth," did not fully work. Once the black middle class emerged, educated and successful, they often preferred to maintain and enjoy personally acquired privileges and no longer wanted to risk fragile acceptance of mainline society by standing in solidarity with the masses of disadvantaged brothers and sisters.

Finally, the Israelites suffered the loss of ethnic entrepreneurial esteem, doing too well—for too long—on someone else's turf. The Hebrews tried to harvest dreams in someone else's field. African-Americans may be given extended privileges of grace by friendly providers for a season. However, sentiments toward minorities' presence in America will change for the worse, when well-doing does not lead us out of dependent economic relationships into the mutuality of self-sufficiency.

I am personally troubled by African-Americans who complete their education and seem more interested in "getting good jobs" rather than "starting their own businesses." Long-term vision is essential to lead African-Americans toward building a strong economic base for the sake of leveraging particular minority interests in the larger society. African-Americans cannot be content with doing well on someone else's turf. The larger society will always assume the right to define possibilities according to their benefit, not necessarily to ours. Start doing well for your primary benefit on someone else's turf and the winds will change on you. The sky is the limit when you find and work on your own turf.

The Hebrews at one time enjoyed Egypt as the land of immense opportunity and prosperity. However, it turned into a wasteland of human oppression and cruel bondage. What happened? A systematic conspiracy of power aggression on the part of the Egyptians aided by the Hebrews' eroded sense of sacred personhood and purpose. What a potent formula for the creation of a living hell!

How do African-Americans survive the soured dream, the hellish nightmare? Here again the biblical Exodus account gives clues for an "ascent from the mire." First, African-Americans must be healed of sinful and hellish tendencies obtained through deep internal reassessment. We must confess, *repenting* of our ways, and address our complicity in creating oppressive conditions. Honesty is required, and taking responsibility for sins contributing to our bondage.

It is essential for African-Americans to *remember who* we are and *whose* we are in our reestablishing of godly identity. The African-American church elders of earlier years of slavery and second-class citizenship often reminded themselves of their first-class status with God by singing that old hymn "I Know I Am a Child of God."

African-Americans need to *reclaim* the God-given values and principles affirming us as a people, again declaring the characteristics which distinguish and bear witness to our relationship with God. God set the Hebrews apart for a holy purpose, to be a unique people, representing him. God never intended for his children to become Egyptians.

Once African-Americans unload oppressive baggage, a *renewed* sense of personhood and purpose for life is crucial. It is vital to African-American survival to raise our minds from the dungeons of oppression and be living witnesses to others of transcending hope. So, even in the midst of a living hell, in some strange way we are called to be heavenly minded.

In addition to internal remedies, external communal actions must also be taken. Difficult times demand *reorganizing* a disorganized African-American people, eliminating dysfunctional programs and disenfranchised resources, and discarding the oppressors' established patterns. African-American people need to implement a restructuring of ourselves for the progressive welfare of our community and its life-affirming interests. Old, inefficient ways need to be tossed out for fresh and enabling avenues of development. Moses organized Israel for the journey to the promised land and led them out.

Then, African-American people must *rely* upon the power of God to liberate. The Hebrews had to be ready when God moved to deliver. God's agenda always included getting his children out of hell. When personal and corporate preparations for liberation are accomplished, then we can look, in faith, for the God who moves in mysterious and powerful ways. He will chart the course and clear the path for African-Americans. The witness of the Bible and the black experience verify that God is moved by our suffering and will open closed doors. "Go down, Moses, way down in Egypt land. Tell ole Pharaoh, let my people go."

Finally, it is critical for African-Americans to *resume* pilgrimage toward the promise of God, avoiding the dangerous illusions of the temporal and terrestrial. It is time to bypass the mirages of materialism, detour around others' versions of the promised land, and get on with our journey. Beyond Egyptian hellholes and wilderness wanderings, God is leading us to a place of God's own choosing, divinely prepared, amply supplied, forever reserved—a place which satisfies eternal longings. For God will be there and our souls shall find their rest in God. The African-American's life journey is not from heaven to hell, but through hell to heaven. It is a journey well worth making.

But until African-Americans reach this blessed homeland of the soul, O sons and daughters of Africa, children of God, and joint heirs with our Lord Jesus Christ, let our aim be upward. For "We are climbing Jacob's ladder" and "every round goes higher, higher." Let us march onward, echoing the musical wisdom of our sainted foreparents who sang with blessed determination:

> We're on our way to Canaan land
> We're on our way to Canaan land
> We're on our way to Canaan land
> We're on our way, praise God!
> We're on our way. ✛

Going Beyond News From the Brickyard

Exodus 5:1–9, 15–23; 6:1

Edward L. Wheeler (B.A., Morehouse College; M.Div., Colgate Rochester Divinity School; Ph.D., Emory University) is Dean of the Chapel at Tuskegee University in Tuskegee Institute, Alabama.

Edward L. Wheeler

Going Beyond News From the Brickyard

Afterward Moses and Aaron went to Pharaoh and said, "Thus says the LORD, the God of Israel, 'Let my people go, that they may hold a feast to me in the wilderness.'" But Pharaoh said, "Who is the LORD, that I should heed his voice and let Israel go? I do not know the LORD, and moreover I will not let Israel go." Then they said, "The God of the Hebrews has met with us; let us go, we pray, a three days' journey into the wilderness, and sacrifice to the LORD our God, lest he fall upon us with pestilence or with the sword." But the king of Egypt said to them, "Moses and Aaron, why do you take the people away from their work? Get to your burdens." And Pharaoh said, "Behold, the people of the land are now many and you make them rest from their burdens!" The same day Pharaoh commanded the taskmasters of the people and their foremen, "You shall no longer give the people straw to make bricks, as heretofore; let them go and gather straw for themselves. But the number of bricks which they made heretofore you shall lay upon them, you shall by no means lessen it; for they are idle; therefore they cry, 'Let us go and offer sacrifice to our God.' Let heavier work be laid upon the men that they may labor at it and pay no regard to lying words." Then the foremen of the people of Israel came and cried to Pharaoh, "Why do you deal thus with your servants? No straw is given to your servants, yet they say to us, 'Make bricks!' And behold, your servants are beaten; but the fault is in your own people." But he said, "You are idle, you are idle; therefore you say, 'Let us go and sacrifice to the LORD.' Go now, and work; for no straw shall be given you, yet you shall deliver the same number of bricks." The foremen of the people of Israel saw that they were in evil plight, when they said, "You shall by no means lessen your daily number of bricks." They met Moses and Aaron, who were waiting for them, as they came forth from Pharaoh; and they said to them, "The Lord look upon you and judge, because you have made us offensive in the sight of Pharaoh and his servants, and have put a sword in their hand to kill us."

Then Moses turned again to the LORD and said, "O LORD, why hast thou done evil to this people? Why didst thou ever send me? For since I came to Pharaoh to speak in thy name, he has done evil to this people, and thou hast not delivered thy people at all." But the LORD said to Moses, "Now you shall see what I will do to Pharaoh; for with a strong hand he will send them out, yea, with a strong hand he will drive them out of his land" (EXODUS 5:1–9, 15–23; 6:1 RSV).

Some time ago ABC television made network history by airing a show entitled "Being Black in White America." African-American persons on ABC's staff reported, directed and produced the telecast. No single television program can tell the multi-faceted and complex story of African-American people, yet this program did a good job of indicating the pride and problems of black people.

The telecast proved valuable, although it seemed to end on an unsure note, leaving the audience in doubt concerning the outcome of the terrible struggles faced by the African-American community. I found very little in it to reassure myself of the possibilities for African-American survival.

I appreciate that ABC saw the need to objectively and honestly communicate the despair prevalent among African-Americans. However, I want to deliver another message, not grounded in negative statistics (such as, over 50 percent of African-American children are born to unwed mothers, African-American males comprise only 6 percent of the U. S. population, 40 percent are incarcerated, etc.) about African-Americans. My message is based on certain Scriptures which continue to remind African-American people that God's actions are not limited by the bad news prevalent in our day.

The passage in Exodus opens with an interesting and curious scene. Moses, the shepherd from Midian and former fugitive from Egyptian justice, along with his brother Aaron, came before the Pharaoh. They are demanding, on behalf of the God of Israel, that Pharaoh let the Israelite slaves go to celebrate a feast to God in the wilderness. However, Israelite slaves were important to Pharaoh because they made bricks for their Egyptian oppressors.

That epitomizes the dehumanizing nature of slavery itself: the bricks the Israelites made were used to build monuments to Egyptian dominance and power. This reinforced the idea that the ways of the Egyptians reigned superior to those of the brick-making slave.

Moses' request struck at the very heart of what it meant to be a slave. The brickyard symbolized both Egyptian power and slave powerlessness. Whatever happened in the brickyard affected everything else in Egypt. If slaves in the brickyard were freed, everything in Egypt would be forced to change. Therefore, Moses' request understandably generated several reactions. I have identified these responses as "news from the brickyard."

1. PHARAOH'S RESPONSE

Moses and Aaron addressed their demands to Pharaoh, the all-powerful head of the most advanced society of the day. Moses did not impress Pharaoh with his request, instead, Pharaoh asked, "Who is the LORD that I should obey His voice and let Israel go?" Pharaoh went on to say that he did not know the Lord and would not release the Hebrew slaves. As a matter of fact, Pharaoh was so unimpressed with Moses and his God that he told the taskmasters and slave foremen to make the slaves gather their own straw for the bricks and not to lessen the quota of bricks they must produce.

Pharaoh heard the demands of God through Moses but totally ignored them. He responded by increasing the work expected from the slaves working in the brickyard. As master over the brickyard he refused to relinquish any of the power and authority he believed he had. Pharaoh thought that he really was in charge and therefore he did not need to have any regard for God or the slaves of the brickyard.

The world we live in does not recognize God. This is one of the harshest realities of modern times and a very sad fact. Many national leaders claim to know God, yet act in ways totally contrary to his mandates. National leaders use their countries' resources to satisfy the greed of a few, rather than showing concern for those at the bottom of life's ladder, the downtrodden, oppressed, and poor. The cries of the hungry are ignored, while those in authority build weapons of destruction. The children of the brickyard receive a poor education in our society, then the same society says "damn them" for not being as good as privileged children. The demand for justice falls on the deaf ears. The world does not know or care about God. Therefore, most people overlook God's warnings about the treatment of widows and orphans.

Christians ought not to be surprised. Sin always seeks its own way and believes it is in charge and has a right to rule without regard for God. Sin consistently makes individuals and societies think they can ignore God and do whatever they want to do. And, sad to say, all too often it appears that Pharaoh, the world, and sin are indeed the real rulers of the world.

The news from Pharaoh regarding the brickyard was not good. He would not let the slaves go and would increase the work they were to do. In our world the Pharaohs still ignore good and heap more burdens on the backs of those least able to carry the load.

2. The People's Response

At first, the Hebrews of the brickyard received Moses' message of deliverance with enthusiasm and gratitude to God. However, the people possessed a shallow faith. The children of Israel wanted freedom from the brickyard without any personal struggle. They failed to count the cost of liberation. Therefore, when Pharaoh increased their work load, the slaves got mad at Moses and Aaron for upsetting the Pharaoh and making matters tougher on them. How ironic. Instead of getting mad at Pharaoh for his cruelty to the slaves and his failure to obey God, the slaves got upset with the ones trying to secure their freedom.

Things among the slaves in the brickyard had gotten so bad that they cared more about Pharaoh's thoughts and his opinions concerning them than God's feelings about their existence as slaves. The slaves did not want to run the risk of offending Pharaoh.

How similar this sounds to African-Americans today. People claim to want liberation but fail to understand that freedom from any kind of oppression requires sacrifice and work. Sinners cannot be free from sin without saying "yes" to Christ. Brickyard people who would be free from the brickyard must be willing to understand who they are and stop making excuses for not being the best they can be.

Many people—black, white, red, and yellow—claim they want to be free from the brickyard of poverty and second-class treatment. Even as they wait for God to act, however, they fail to realize that succumbing to the pressure exerted by their peers to act in a certain way will make leaving the brickyard even harder.

People struggling to survive in the brickyard do not understand that their value is not based on what Pharaoh says about them but on the fact that they are God's children. Some individuals become accustomed to being slaves and are unwilling to sacrifice in the name of freedom. Slaves stripped of their sense of worth and value look to their oppressor for personal confirmation, dismissing and rejecting the messengers of God. They mistakenly believe their freedom will come without a struggle.

How often have you and I accepted sin, second-class treatment, and the pain of the brickyard, thinking it's too much trouble to change our lives for the better? How often have we accepted less than what God has in store for us because we were more concerned about the opinions of those around us than the opinion of God? How often have we been guilty of initially cheering the news about our freedom only to get mad when we learned liberty requires personal sacrifice?

3. MOSES' RESPONSE

Pharaoh rejected Moses' demand to free the slaves in the brickyard. The brickyard slaves complained about the additional work as a result of Moses' request. Moses is confident God called him to deliver the people, but the opposition depressed and upset him.

Moses complained to God, "God, you have not kept your promise to the children of Israel." The Moses who boldly stood before Pharaoh is now broken and fearful. He is not sure God will do what he promised he would do. Moses began to doubt God and his role as the people's liberator. Consequently, he started paying too much attention to the hopeless brickyard news.

Christians beginning to doubt also are guilty of taking too much interest in the brickyard news, whether God can set the slaves free. We hear so much about the drop-out rate, teen illiteracy, drug/alcohol addiction, and teenage pregnancy that we throw up our hands, concluding that there is nothing anybody can do to change the situation. Increasingly, people disregard the church and disrespect moral values. We are tempted to write off a whole generation of youth, consigning them to life in the brickyard. Sins in our society have become so brazen and bold that many people doubt if things can be turned around. Some of us simply want to be left alone.

I want to tell you today, the brickyard news is not the final word, so don't despair. After Pharaoh had his say, the slaves complained, and Moses doubted, then God spoke. He restated his commitment to set the people free, "MY WORD *is* the final WORD." God always has the final say, exerting his ultimate authority. No matter what the situation may appear to be, only God's perspective counts. If God says the captives will be freed, they will be freed. Neither sin, Pharaohs, crosses, tombs, Red Seas, injustice, slavery, crack, racism, poverty, ghetto high-rises, slum-lords, unemployment, oppression, Supreme Court setbacks, nor program cutbacks can keep us from being free. God sides with the brickyard residents; he delivers the oppressed and hears the cry of the downtrodden.

The news about African-Americans as a people may not be good. Many doubt our survival, but I am not one of them. I believe God will deliver us if we dare to go beyond the news from the brickyard and "Hold to God's Unchanging Hand." ✚

The Walls Came Tumbling Down

Joshua 6:20

Charles L. Dinkins (A.B., Oberlin College; B.D., Oberlin Graduate School of Theology; M.Div., Vanderbilt University) is pastor of the First Baptist Church Lauderdale in Memphis, Tennessee.

The Walls Came Tumbling Down

So the people shouted, and the trumpets were blown. As soon as the people heard the sound of the trumpet, the people raised a great shout, and the wall fell down flat, so that the people went up into the city, every man straight before him, and they took the city (JOSHUA 6:20 RSV).

This message is taken from the story of Joshua leading the children of Israel into the Promised Land. Moses commissioned Joshua to lead the Israelites into the land because God did not permit him to enter. All of the people who left Egypt under Moses' leadership died before reaching the Promised Land, except Joshua and Caleb. God spared those two men because they brought back a favorable report after spying out the new land.

Before going into Canaan, Joshua sent spies into the area to see what Israel faced once across the Jordan River. The spies stopped in Jericho, the first city in Canaan, entering the house of Rahab, the Harlot. She befriended them and hid them from the officials of Jericho.

The spies reported back to Joshua and he organized the Israelites to cross the Jordan and battle for Jericho. Once a day for six days, the people marched around Jericho's city walls. They marched seven times on the seventh day. The priest blew the trumpets signaling the Israelites to shout. And the walls came tumbling down!

Joshua's story proves valuable for African-Americans today. We can draw several lessons from Joshua's experience which are applicable to the present.

Recently, a considerable amount of attention has been focused on African-American history. Most people know the events occurring from the time of slavery until the present.

We've observed the walls come down on slavery, segregation (legal, that is), voting rights, civil rights, public accommodations access, progress in education, jobs, and quality of life. African-Americans used "ramrods" to knock these walls down, one by one. Invisible walls still exist, however. Barricades in the hearts of people discriminate and pre-judge. Subtle bigotry remains in the area of employment opportunities and access to financial resources.

Joshua's experience relates to four issues African-Americans are facing today.

1. LEADERSHIP

Notice the orderly process of leadership transition from Moses to Joshua. He caught the spirit of Moses, and his predecessor exposed him to excellent training. Joshua accompanied Moses to Mount Sinai when the people fashioned the Golden Calf. He took charge of the first tent meeting of the Children of Israel in the wilderness. Moses chose Joshua, along with eleven others, to spy out the land in Canaan and report back concerning its vulnerability. Joshua joined Caleb in attempting to persuade the people to move forward and take the Promised Land. Because of their faith in God's promises, he spared their lives. Joshua and Caleb entered the Promised Land, the only original link with Israel's past history in Egypt. The rest of the first generation died in the wilderness. Moses ordained Joshua to be his successor and to continue to lead the people. Moses saw the Promised Land from the mountain, but God did not allow him to enter.

In Moses' and Joshua's times God required a single leader. God, the real leader, needed someone to communicate his instructions to the people. Currently, numerous persons and organizations seek to lead African-American people, but no "Moses" exists in the NAACP, not in the Urban League or SCLC or any other organization, not even in the Rainbow Coalition. We fight battles on many fronts, with a variety of objectives and goals, but no single leader has emerged to galvanize us. The further away we get from the walls of legal segregation, the more African-Americans appear to be a leaderless people.

Even Martin Luther King, Jr., a spokesman for the ambitions and hopes of black people, did not operate alone. A cadre of persons mobilized on behalf of his programs. King is the closest to a leader the African-American race has seen in recent years.

Now, you might ask, do white people have a leader? The answer is "No." Even the President of the United States will be opposed and questioned. On some things, such as foreign policy, Republicans and Democrats might come together. But domestic issues cause division. However, white people maintain one advantage: their network of country and civic clubs, trade associations and labor unions, and cultural groups. Their economic goals are expressed through Chambers of Commerce; their social programs through organizations like the United Way. Government officials speak out, mold opinions, and stimulate discussions on their behalf. The Caucasian race owns a network of media communications (which also reach African-Americans) and other systems organized to serve their needs. This kind of "power" is hard to fight.

In the African-American community we participate in church organizations and denominations, associations, and social clubs. When we get together, what do we talk about? Are our groups being used effectively to galvanize opinion? *Ebony* magazine annually lists the top one hundred most influential African-Americans. Over ninety percent are constituency based, and the names of the leaders are the only thing changing each year. *Ebony* lists the same fraternities and sororities, political and church groups, civil rights organizations, and lodges year after year. African-Americans do not control the capacity to shift *capital about to serve our needs*. When a program or project requires finances, the money must be "raised."

We talk about the churches' influence, but people possess more money in their personal bank accounts than there is in the churches' treasuries. Church members restrict the leadership by concerning themselves with who controls the finances. Because African-Americans regulate such a limited number of establishments, there is a struggle for leadership in the churches. The battles white people fight in Chambers of Commerce and political organizations, African-Americans dispute in fraternities, sororities, lodges, and even in the church.

African-Americans need leadership to unify the people and organize individuals to address various issues. An organized people is a great asset.

This leadership also needs to know how to command resources and manage money both appropriately and quickly in order to respond to the numerous needs of African-Americans. Effectiveness in administration of people depends on appropriate supervision of resources.

African-Americans know how to manage survival, but what about prosperity? Ownership in the community needs to be spread around. African-Americans own "not-for-profit" things. Assets are not being developed in "not-for-profit" institutions. Someone said that a city like Memphis requires only four or five African-American millionaires who can organize our financial resources in order to greatly enhance the community.

We must educate for leadership. Mature leaders who train new authority figures about how to use resources effectively are necessary for an orderly leadership transition. Every time leadership steps down it's a waste of time for new leaders to go back to square one. Joshua experienced a smooth transition. Moses prepared and trained him and he easily took the superior role. Leaders in the African-American community need to follow Moses' example.

2. INTELLIGENCE

Intelligence is usually thought of in terms of the ability to perceive and comprehend meaning, adapt to one's environment,

Living in Hell

learn from experience, and seize the essential factors of a complex matter. But I prefer to think of *intelligence* in the military sense: the collection of secret information.

There is *public information* and there is *private information*. If you are going to make a good decision, you require the necessary information. Joshua sent two spies into Jericho. Where did they go? To the public library? To educational institutions, media, books, or research? No! The spies looked for private information at the house of a harlot.

Now, I'm not suggesting that is where you should get information today. However, if you want information, you need to go where you can get the facts. People considered Rahab's house a common place to find foreign and local persons openly discussing city activities and secrets. The spies learned there that the people of Jericho feared the Hebrews and their God.

African-Americans struggle for access to everything one considers a part of the good American life: cars, schools, jobs, skills, clothes, vacations, etc. As African-Americans gain more access, which include promotions, we learn more about what is going on and what makes the world around us tick. Some African-Americans know the location of resources and are in a position to look over and see how things work. However, they are unable to shift these resources around to their advantage. African-Americans do not command the board rooms—not yet. The meeting place where important influential decisions are discussed and executed still remains a white male bastion.

I read a story in *Lear's* magazine which said that this nation will not reach its fullest potential until women are in the board rooms. One might add to that statement: not until African-Americans are in the board rooms.

What drives this country is economics: the production, distribution, and consumption of wealth. Money can be appropriated from profits made through supplying the material needs of people. African-Americans mostly are consumers. Yet we know the value of distribution, entrepreneurship, and making money.

The demand is to move toward production ownership. African-Americans work, make money, and spend it while watching other people put their money together, massage it, and invest it. For example, no major stock-owned African-American business has been formed in Memphis since Tri-State Bank organized in 1946. Black folks have money. Just look at the things we *buy!*

African-Americans think in terms of organizing people by looking to *politics* as a way out. But politics is just one part of the equation. Politics must be financed. Candidates for public office need money to run. People select public officials by supporting candidates. Candidates the people do not want are generally unable to raise money. This has nothing to do with their right to run, or their ability.

African-American political advances are obvious. Mississippi, a state sweltering under the heat of oppression, holds the largest number of African-American elected officials in the nation. In fact, it appears whites gave some positions to African-Americans, then set invisible political walls barring us from any more. A new breed of African-American politician knows that "access to money" is the key to political progress and building coalition intelligence. This is the information necessary to make decisions. How do you get money? And how do you use money? By *intelligence*. Finding out where it is: learning about the resources of private and public sectors affecting the community.

3. PLANNING

Jericho was the first city the Israelites reached upon entering the Promised Land. It was a strategic protected city, with walls like fortresses, gates to control ingress and egress, and sentries and spies to observe who came in and went out. Surely, security kept an eye on the activities at Rahab's house. With this information, their intelligence officers planned defenses and controlled what went on inside the city walls. Strangers walking the streets of Jericho underwent investigation.

Joshua knew God promised the Israelites the victory but he needed a strategic plan. This is what Joshua told the people:

1. Follow the priests who carry the covenant box of the Lord. This is new ground we are entering. (In the past, the African-American church led into new ground: institutions, civil rights, and now economics. Needs are to be identified and supplied.)

2. Purify yourselves—not only as individuals, but also as a group. Get your bodies and your minds right; clean up physically, mentally, and emotionally. (The African-American race cannot make it with so many folks on drugs, in prison, or caught in socially unproductive behavior.)

When the toes of the priests touched the water in the Jordan River, the waters divided so the people could move into Canaan. (Leaders and followers in the African-American church must move to the same step if they are to be successful. It is important to organize resources and move toward self-esteem. We find many people desiring to take charge of situations but African-Americans must seize control over their own destiny. Then if others want to help, fine.)

3. Plan a strategy and organize the people. (No one is afraid of disorganized folk. Their efforts will eventually fall apart. It is important for people to learn where they can contribute and to recognize the contributions of others.)

In church groups, African-Americans often focus on *how many* and *how much*. It's time to go beyond this limited stage and develop strategies for training people how to invest their capital and stop begging for what we do not possess. Some things African-Americans ought to continue fighting for; however, some things we've already obtained. The church needs to help individuals plan and make use of previous advances.

I talked with several business people who want loans, but what they need are investments—loans versus equity. Can business leaders sell their proposition in order for someone to willingly "go in with them?" God asked Moses, "What do you have in your hand?" What do African-Americans hold in their hands:

education, intellect, money? Put it together! Kenneth Gibson, former mayor of Newark, New Jersey, said something like this: "When African-American people left that inner city for life in the suburbs, organizations and communications fractured. Education, money, and intelligence—all left." The community's recovery and advancement depend upon finances and know-how. *African-Americans must organize and use their potential.*

4. TOGETHERNESS

Joshua organized the people. The priests with the trumpets marched and led the people around the wall. Jericho's locked gates did not allow outside people entrance into the city. Israel owned no battering rams to break the gates open. They marched around the city—one, two, three, four, five—six whole days.

The people of Jericho heard the trumpets and the sounds of Israel parading, but nothing happened. Jericho's citizens felt confident and secure. People are not afraid of noise. This is a noisy world.

Then came day seven. The number seven was considered sacred among the Israelites. God created the earth in six days, but he rested on the seventh day, set it apart and declared it holy. On that day, Joshua told the people to march around the walls seven times in cadence and formation. The Israelites marched in unity, right foot up, left foot down, shaking the ground around Jericho's fortress. The vibrations caused the mortar to loosen and the stones to start trembling. When the trumpet blew, the people shouted, causing more vibrations, and the walls came tumbling down. The army moved in and captured the city.

The "physical walls" are falling. Gradually, the barriers separating African-Americans from the good life are breaking down. *Invisible walls still remain*:

- We have systems to deal with criminals, but crime still remains.

- We passed laws to ensure access to whatever others have access to, on the same terms, but prejudice still remains.
- We set up welfare systems to give the poor what the public determines are the minimum necessities for survival, but poverty still remains.
- We build systems of education (schools, colleges, universities) and libraries, but ignorance still remains.
- We build the means of production, to satisfy the growing needs of people, but lack of skills and unemployment still remain.
- We identify *problems* one by one and solve them, but *issues* still remain.
- We enhance the quality of life and extend the length of life, but death still remains.

Only God is able to penetrate the hidden divisions and make the walls tumble down. He alone can rid our society of prejudice, selfishness, and greed.

The answer to the problem comes from Joshua: "Follow the Lord and he will give you victory" (Joshua 1:8, paraphrased). God has traveled with African-American people throughout our history. He led us over rough places, gave us friends at the right times, held bowed-down heads high, and gave hope. God will be with *us* now.

Spread the word about God. Let the world know about him. God is to be credited with all our achievements. If we embrace God and follow him, *the walls will tumble down.* One by one African-Americans have witnessed enemies wiped out. New opposition against black people constantly arises to replace the old judgmental attitudes and discriminatory actions. But in time the new opposition will crumble too. We have seen racists who swore by the word "Never," confident that the civil rights movement would fail, have to change their tune.

If African-Americans keep their hands in God's hand, we can move into the Promised Land. The walls will fall, and we can move on to the next struggle. ✢

You Already Have It!

Judges 6:12–16

Reginald L. Porter, Sr. (B.S., University of Memphis; M.Div., Memphis Theological Seminary; D.Min., Eastern Baptist Seminary) is pastor of the Greenwood Missionary Baptist Church in Tuskegee Institute, Alabama.

You Already Have It!

The angel of the LORD showed himself to Gideon and said, "You are a brave man, and the LORD is with you." Gideon said, "But pray, my lord, if the LORD really is with us, why has all this happened to us? What has become of all those wonderful deeds of his, of which we have heard from our fathers, when they told us how the LORD brought us out of Egypt? But now the LORD has cast us off and delivered us into the power of the Midianites." The LORD turned to him and said, "Go and use this strength of yours to free Israel from the power of the Midianites. It is I that send you." Gideon said, "Pray, my lord, how can I serve Israel? Look at my clan: it is the weakest in Manasseh, and I am the least of my father's family." The LORD answered, "I will be with you, and you shall lay low all Midian as one man" (JUDGES 6:12–16 NEB).

The stories of the Old Testament hold a special place in the affections of African-American people, especially the historical accounts about the oppression and deliverance of the children of Israel. In these narratives about the God of the universe dealing with Israel, African-American people find comfort, strength, and an inexhaustible source of hope. How exciting it is for an oppressed people to hear repeatedly, "When all seems lost, God will step in and save his own." His ways are sometimes confusing and he tests the faith the strongest believer, but God never fails. He never abandons his own! I want African-Americans to take a close look at this exciting story of deliverance.

The familiar story about Gideon is one Old Testament gem touching the spirit of the downcast. The tense drama unfolds in the book of Judges, as God prepares Gideon and his army for battle. The drama peaks as the Lord in his own time uses unmistakable tactics, leading the army on to victory.

The Midianites sorely oppressed God's people, who suffered greatly. The enemy confiscated their crops and herds with no regard for the Israelites' survival. "They [Midianites] then pitched their camps in the country and destroyed the crops as far as the outskirts of Gaza, leaving nothing to support life in Israel, sheep or ox . . ." (Judges 6:4).

This sounds like the plight of American cities, which are becoming increasingly African-American. A trip through any city reveals crumbled buildings that once housed thriving small businesses, closed factories, boarded-up houses, abandoned schools, and even graffiti-covered structures that used to be churches. These are all signs the oppressors entered, with little consideration for the residents. Those who do not care about the welfare of people in the city take away all the good, leaving inadequate supplies to sustain life in any form. When physical signs of oppression are present, the emotional and psychological companions are not far behind! Those who live under another's heel experience paranoia, self-hatred, hopelessness, self-doubt, anger, despair, and rage.

It is not hard to figure out why the African-American community reeks with hypertension, drug abuse, mistrust, and crime. Living under oppression is like "living in hell." If you are in hell, nothing else matters.

In the midst of this type of situation, we meet Gideon. He is threshing wheat for food. He works in haste, fearfully hiding from the Midianites. If he is discovered, it could mean hunger or perhaps even his life. The angel of the Lord appears to Gideon, greeting him, "You are a brave man, and the Lord is with you." How strange. A brave man in seclusion. What an odd salute for a person working fearfully in secret.

I wonder if brave men hide today?
Are strong men and women, full of potential, working in
    haste and secrecy, because they are frightened of the
    wrath of the opposition?

They know what needs to be said and done,
but are paralyzed with anxiety,
scared of losing their jobs, homes, grades, promotions,
    or status.

Petrified people thinking someone will retaliate against
    their children.
Potentially great people cowering because the limited
    freedom they enjoy may be taken away or they see the
    powerful arsenal of weapons owned by the ones on the
    other side.

Where are they hiding?
Check the street corners, look into the alleys,
scope out the crack houses,
peer into the bars,
peek behind the dead bolts,
visit the jails,
and you will find them.
But do not stop there.
Go into fine restaurants or exclusive clubs;
step into corporate board rooms or fancy office buildings;
ride through the suburbs of the good side of town;
walk, if you dare, into the sanctuary of far too many
    churches;
and you will find them hiding.

Like Gideon, strong African-American men and women conceal themselves because of fear! Like this Old Testament character, the fear of those today is rooted in years of experience as persons who do not count. Gideon's encounter with God presents a piercing bit of good news for those feeling insignificant and who are in seclusion. *God knows who you are and where you are!* What a joy! What a powerful word! God knows the real you and your potential. He placed it inside of you. Others may discount and dismiss you as nothing. In spite of forced circumstances, God knows where to find you. He will come, acknowledging your capabilities and assuring you of his presence. The angel says to Gideon, you are a hero in hiding. "You are a brave man, and the Lord is with you."

Gideon's response to the angel is an example of what frequently happens when people are granted a heavenly audience. Gideon wastes precious time raising useless questions and complaining. Why are things the way they are?

When will you do something about my problems? If the Lord is with us, why is life so hard? If Christians approached the throne of God with more praise and thanksgiving and less complaining, it would revolutionize our worship and our lives.

The children of God believe their lives should be free from difficulty, hardship, and struggle. I am convinced the cries filling our prayers are based on this erroneous expectation. Nothing could be further from the truth. Woe to those distorters of the Gospel proclaiming this warped doctrine. I pray those who are misled or simply misunderstood will come to the light. Adversities are woven into the fabric of life. No one escapes them. The witness of Scripture does not support the belief that life is a bed of roses for believers. The Word is loud and clear, however, that in the midst of the uncertainties and the turmoil of life, GOD IS THERE. There is little, if any, benefit in griping, but refreshment and renewal come through communion with God, who is present in the midst of our circumstances.

I must add an important footnote here: although struggle is built into our lives, that does not justify an evil person's preying upon the defenseless, the poor, or the weak. Woe to people who oppress! Misfortune will visit the ungodly! The day of reckoning is surely coming!

One of the most devastating by-products of oppression is the annihilation of self-esteem, along with its feelings of powerlessness and frustration. The dialogue between Gideon and the angel reveals what I mean. The angel, after calling him brave and strong, now tells Gideon to use his strength to free the Israelites. "Go and use this strength of yours to free Israel [and yourself] from the power of the Midianites."

Oh, the plight of the oppressed! They are full of potential, yet hiding, waiting, watching, hoping, praying for someone to deliver them. You already have what is needed to gain freedom!

> Go on Rosa Parks and sit down,
> Your tired feet and strong will are all you need.
> Go on George Washington Carver and discover,
> Your peanut and ingenuity are all you need.
> Go on and sing Mahalia Jackson,
> Your voice and a bit of soul are all you need.
> Build your empire John Johnson,
> Your determination and commitment are all you need.
> Go on black engineers, carpenters, playwrights, doctors,
>   teachers, mechanics, sanitation workers, lawyers, nurse's
>   aides, mothers, fathers,
> Work together.
> SET PEOPLE FREE!
>
> Stop waiting on the government to finally do right.
> Quit depending on the kindness of a few well-meaning
>   souls.
> Don't look for someone else to do the job God has equipped
>   you for.
> GO USE THE STRENGTH YOU HAVE AND SET THE
>   PEOPLE FREE.

Now I must hasten to say, this is not an endorsement of the "self-made man" theory of human development. Gifts and talents will only shine when given proper opportunity. The underdogs are often unjustly denied the chance to display God-given abilities. This injustice must be corrected and not forgotten.

Come out of hiding! Use your gifts. Tap into your hidden potential, including the most powerful resource of all—God's promise. His commitment to those who come out fighting is this: "I will be with you." God will open doors and create opportunities, even if it means soundly defeating the Midianites.

Gideon's response to the angel's challenge reflects his feelings of futility and inadequacy, bred by a repressive situation. The down-and-outer devalues himself, his family, and his chances. "What can I do?" "I'm nothing." "I come from a nothing family." "I'm the least of my insignificant clan." "What can I possibly do?" How many times have you heard it said? "My vote won't count." "I don't have enough education." "I don't go to a big church." "My husband is not like your husband." "But you know how it is in this neighborhood." "I don't talk good enough." "She has the right clothes to wear, I don't." "Nothing I do will matter." "I don't have what it takes." THE LIST IS ENDLESS.

The Lord's answer to Gideon and all frightened, burdened people is this: "I WILL BE WITH YOU." God's presence makes up for whatever is lacking in abilities or possessions. His closeness (not our abilities) is the difference between victory and defeat. He multiplies strength.

God goes on to tell Gideon, "You shall lay low all Midian as one man." Can one man really make a difference? Can one woman truly dent the armor of the enemy? The story of Gideon's incredible victory suggests that one individual following God's lead can surely make a difference.

"Oh sure," you respond, "That happened in the Bible, thousands of years ago. What about now? Can one person standing in the face of overwhelming odds still make a difference?" God's war against oppression did not stop with one victory. Look up the historical record of men and women daring to stand up instead of hiding. Read the names of Samson, Daniel, Esther, John the Baptist, and the apostle Paul. But don't stop with the biblical record, for God continues to march across the pages of recorded time. Find the names of Harriet Tubman, Sojourner Truth, Ida B. Wells, and Barbara Jordan. Read the witness of Frederick Douglass, Mahatma Ghandi, Malcolm X, Martin Luther King, and Nelson Mandela. The same God who spoke, commissioned, and went ahead of these brave individuals of the past still sends angels into obscure places today. He is still saying, "Go use the strength I've already given to set the people free."

To all who answer God's call, he gives this assurance, "I WILL BE WITH YOU." African-Americans marching in the streets of America in the fifties and sixties seemed to understand. In the midst of their protest against oppression they continuously said, "The Lord is on our side.... We shall overcome!" ✢

Living in Hell: The Need for a Man in the Black Family

2 Kings 4:1–3; 6–7

Reuben H. Green (B.A., Bishop College; B.D., Oberlin Graduate School of Theology; S.T.M., Iliff School of Theology; D.Min., Vanderbilt University Graduate School of Theology) is pastor of the Central Baptist Church in Memphis, Tennessee.

Reuben H. Green

Living in Hell: The Need for a Man in the Black Family

Now there cried a certain woman of the wives of the prophets unto Elisha, saying, Thy servant my husband is dead; and thou knowest that thy servant did fear the LORD: and the creditor is come to take unto him my two sons to be bondmen. And Elisha said unto her, What shall I do for thee? tell me, what hast thou in the house? And she said, Thine handmaid hath not any thing in the house, save a pot of oil. Then he said, Go, borrow thee vessels abroad of all thy neighbors, even empty vessels; borrow not a few. . . . And it came to pass, when the vessels were full, that she said unto her son, Bring me yet a vessel. And he said unto her, There is not a vessel more. And the oil stayed. Then she came and told the man of God. And he said, Go, sell the oil, and pay thy debt, and live thou and thy children of the rest (2 KINGS 4:1– 3; 6–7 KJV).

Life in America is ambiguous, at best. This ambiguity is evident on the faces of the people who live in this country, regardless of race, financial standing, social status, or religious orientation. What is considered a basic uncertainty for most Americans is viewed as hell for African-Americans. The following incident illustrates the primary ambivalence of young African-Americans.

Recently I spoke at a local high school. As I looked out over the audience, tears filled my eyes because the majority of the students exhibited a spirit of lethargy. I do not believe this demeanor is exhibited because A' an-American boys and girls are lazy or indifferent to the events of our day. I believe it's more deep-seated than mere teenage apathy. This attitude is built on the unfortunate facts that African-American youth do not believe there is anything positive to look forward to in the future.

African-Americans feel like hopeless children possessing no insight into their own existence. Our youth do not know who they are and we have not taken the time to tell them who they are. In fact, youth are told at home and in school that they belong to a race of nobodies. Our young African-Americans are not pointing to black heroes with pride. When one is uncertain of his or her character, any history will do. Welcome to America.

What can we expect when all our African-American children hear in school is somebody else's culture? As early as 1933, Carter G. Woodson told African-Americans, "We are mis-educating our children." He said, "We have taught our children to admire the Hebrews, the Greeks, the Latins, and the Teuton and to despise the African."

A few weeks ago, a concerned parent of an elementary school student gave me a detailed outline of the program that her daughter's school used during the month of February. The first week was dedicated to the war in the Persian Gulf; the second week was Heart Week; the third week was President's Week; and the fourth week was School Loyalty Week. Not one word was spoken about the contributions of African-American people at the school during the month that was dedicated to African-American people by the staff or teachers in the school. We live in hell because our society creates it for us.

To help African-Americans escape from this living hell, I'm offering the following suggestions. On holidays such as Easter, Christmas, the Fourth of July, and birthdays, buy your children books instead of toys. Introduce them to the beauty of words. Limit television and comic-book time. To do less speaks of death in its most lasting form—the slow but efficient erosion of the mind and consignment to hell forever. To do less is to provide for them no exit from this hell.

Let us remember, a mindless people joins rather than initiates, obeys rather than questions, follows rather than leads, begs rather than demands. Unless African-Americans get their minds right, our existence in hell is permanent, a liability to ourselves and to our community.

The kind of family exemplified in 2 Kings is familiar. It is a single-parent family, headed by a female, with two small children. This type of family is a created hell for African-Americans dating back to slavery.

The slaves maintained no control over their lives. Slave families might include two parents in the morning, but before the sun set in the west, the family members might be separated from one another forever. What greater hell is there in this world than to be permanently severed from the fellowship of mother, father, sister, or brother?

This kind of family separation continues in African-American communities. Fathers assume the role of the visiting husband when the welfare worker comes around. The concept of the visiting husband dates back to very ancient times. African-American men support this practice because the economic conditions that this country provides consigns them to a living hell.

The husband of the woman in 2 Kings is associated with the prophetic community called The Sons of the Prophets. The husband had recently died. This widow became a single parent, but not because her husband had abandoned, legally separated from, or divorced her. In spite of her husband's absence, she attempted to raise her two sons in a dignified manner. As a widow she faced economic obligations that she could not meet. This responsibility proved to be an inescapable living hell.

It is a sin and a shame that we ignore the needs and sorrows of people in their everyday experiences. America spends billions of dollars on wars, yet this country cannot provide homes for the homeless, food for the hungry, and clothes for the naked. An entire society lives in hell when motel rooms are cheaper than a hospital room.

This widow woman carried her problem to the place black people have unloaded their anxieties and cares for so long. She carried it to the Preacher Man. The widow felt the prophet, of all people, understood her hellish living conditions. She goes to the prophet and reports her anguish, "The creditor is about to foreclose and take my two sons as slaves." Often preachers deal with problems from different levels of hell: lights about to be cut off, no food in the home, mortgage payments three months past due, or tuition that must be paid before a daughter or son can take final examinations.

During biblical times, the law permitted enslavement of children to pay debts. The prophet felt the mother's concern. He asked her, "What shall I do for you? Do you have anything in the house?" She said to him, "I don't have anything in my house but a pot of oil." He told her to go and borrow all the empty vessels she could, take the oil, and fill up those vessels. When she filled them all up, he directed her to sell the oil, pay her debt, and live off the rest.

The problems this widow experienced indicated her need for a husband and father to provide for the household. In the African-American community the need for a man in the family is extremely great for several reasons.

1. African-Americans are being terrorized at all levels of human involvement. For many years, African-American people lived in hell with no opportunity to elevate ourselves in this country. Our race is often portrayed as chief villains: all of the ills of America could be cured if black people did not usurp the nation's resources. Kill the welfare system and America will progress? What about those rich farmers who are paid millions of dollars not to plant crops on their land? The fear of two African-American men elected George Bush to the presidency of this country in the 1988 election. They were Jesse Jackson and Willie Horton.

The widow in 2 Kings lived in hell because of her poverty and creditors. When you live on meager resources, life consists of what is available or left over from the well-to-do. A legacy from my boyhood days are thoughts of my mother taking leftover biscuits, rice, or beef and making bread pudding, rice pudding, or hash. Mother took what most people toss out as scraps and made a life for her family.

God has supremely blessed the African-American community, and we have made great strides in recent years. We have enough resources to banish sorrow and to bring hope and cheer into the lives of people. I get tired of reading about the latest African-American millionaires. I don't care about Reggie Jackson's cars, Wilt Chamberlain's beds, Diana Ross's houses, Eddie Murphy's parties, or Walter Payton's guns. Where are the rich African-American men who care about the majority of their people, who desire to help the despairing who see no hope of advancement or improvement in their future? We must cease terrorizing ourselves. The task facing African-American men is the development of skills, roles, and means needed for advancing our race.

2. Then, too, there is need for a man in the African-American family today because what Elisha did is within the reach of us all.

Elisha was possessed by God's Holy Spirit. This is available to all Christians. We may all perform deeds of mercy which will seem like miracles in other people's eyes. For example, spending a couple of hours a week being a Big Brother to a lonely boy, tutoring students encountering difficulty in school, lending a helping hand to the half-dead person on a present-day Jericho Road—those may be our twentieth-century miracles.

Elisha took what the woman owned—her oil—and made it useful. The only way African-Americans can increase our resources is to use what we have. Let's not be so tightfisted that nothing will come out of our hands and God cannot put anything in our hands.

The miracles occurred without Elisha's presence. He left something for the woman and her sons to do. This left them with a sense of pride and a feeling that they were doing something to lift themselves out of their living hell. One of the sons brought the empty vessels and the other one set the full vessels aside. We need to teach our children how to work. That's part of our problem.

Traditionally, African-American men reared the children, especially the boys and young men. Fathers passed skills on to their sons. Young African-American men learned to be providers and protectors of their families. That is why it is important that African-American men be involved in the family.

3. A man is needed in the African-American family in order to show young men, by precept and example, the necessity of faith. The writer of the Hebrews said, "Without faith, it is impossible to please God." Faith can move mountains. Jesus said, "If we had the faith of a grain of mustard seed, we could say unto the mountain, 'Be removed from here to there,' and it will remove. So nothing will be impossible to you" (Matthew 17:20 paraphrased). From God all blessing flow. The widow's sons did not see the springs that supplied the oil, but they believed them to be in Him from whom all blessings flow.

God still meets needs and fills vessels today. The more containers placed before him, the more oil he gives. It's up to us to supply the vessels. Our containers are our special God-given talents. If we take our abilities and pour them out in service to others, our supply will never run out. The Master said, "Give, and it will be given to you: good measure, pressed down, shaken together, and running over . . ." (Luke 6:38 NKJV).

The widow's oil multiplied. Oil is a symbol of grace. God observes our present condition. But he doesn't just see our condition; he does something about it. God supplied the prophet for this woman. The man of God knew what to do for her particular problem.

When God does something for you, tell somebody about his goodness. An illustration, given by Dr. Cameron Alexander of Georgia, makes this point very well.

Long before we had these beautiful pipe organs that are mechanically operated, there was a little man called the "Pumper" whose sole function was to get in a box, out of sight of the audience, and pump air for the service. One year the King of Italy came to the village where a concert artist lived. As part of the festivities, a concert was rendered. They sought for the best Pumper there was in the country who happened to reside in this particular village.

The artist had been practicing for forty-five years for this big moment. When the night came for the big concert, the Pumper was promptly stowed away. The artist came out, arched his back, cracked his knuckles, adjusted his seat, and for forty-five minutes played some of the most beautiful music this side of heaven.

At intermission the crowd gave the artist a standing ovation for twenty minutes. When the curtains were drawn and the artist retreated to his dressing room, the little Pumper came from his cage, caught him by the hand and said, "When you come back for the second half of the program, I want you to tell them that I am your Pumper. You don't have to call my name, just introduce me as your Pumper." The artist said, "You must be crazy. Why, I have practiced for over forty-five years for this big event. Do you think that I'm going to let you spoil this moment for me?" The little man said, "I just wish that you would tell them that I am your Pumper."

When the time arrived for the artist to return, he made his way to the organ. He arched his back, cracked his knuckles, adjusted his seat and, with great fanfare, hit the organ. Nothing happened. He thought that maybe he had not done the ritual properly, so he again arched his back, cracked his knuckles, adjusted his seat and, with great fanfare, hit the organ—and, again, nothing happened. The artist reached under the door, caught the little man by the hand, brought him front and center, and said, "Ladies and gentlemen, I want you to meet my Pumper."

Jesus is our Pumper. Let us introduce him to our families. ✢

Be Careful Who You Try to Hang

Esther 7:10

Wyatt Tee Walker (B.S., Virginia Union University; M.Div., Virginia Union University Graduate School of Religion; D.Min., Colgate Rochester University) is senior pastor of the Canaan Baptist Church of Christ in Harlem, New York.

Wyatt Tee Walker

Be Careful Who You Try to Hang

So they hanged Haman on the gallows that he had prepared for

Mordecai . . . (ESTHER 7:10 KJV).

Many things in this life are taken for granted. One fixture in our homes is so much a part of our everyday experience we scarcely take notice. It is called the television. In many homes people own at least one color television (some have two, three or even four). It's common for many to enter the house and flip on the set without even thinking. The T.V. is like a pet or a companion—if we can't watch it, we at least want it on.

The flip of a television switch can bring an image from another part of the world to our homes. We rarely think of how that image comes to be. This is a marvelous technology. Originally a camera photographs an event, such as the Super Bowl. The photograph is broken down into electrical components and runs through a copper wire to a station which bounces the signal from a tall building (transmitting sometimes via satellite). That signal enters the network of our particular city and is run into homes via the antennae. If the television is plugged in to the electrical socket, all we have to do is turn it on. The signal then enters the box, called a television, and inside there is a cobalt plate and a Thompson tube reassembling the electrical components—and we sit there and watch television!

Now with my sanctified imagination, I believe this technology will mature and someday in the distant future we may be able to have an instrument like the television transmitting not only contemporary events, but also telecasting close-ups of past historical events. With one dial we'll be able to select the geographical location, with another button we'll punch in the specific time period, and maybe with a fine-tuning dial we'll tune in the precise time of day.

So, for the purpose of this sermon I want to turn the locus dial to some point near the junction of the Tigris and Euphrates rivers. Then for the time period let's flip to 570 B.C. We will find ourselves in the capital of the Persian Empire, called Shushan. Now let's turn the fine tuning dial to about ten minutes to six in the morning.

As the zoom lens moves in, we see on our screen the great capital of the Persian Empire just beginning to awake. There is that first thin pencil-line of dawn heralding the arrival of a new day, a rush of fragrance in the humid air, the sweet scents of jasmine and narcissus. A lone workman comes down one of the broad avenues leading to the main entrance of the king's palace, decorated with carved lions in a sitting position. As he turns the corner, in his peripheral vision he catches the image of a man hanging from a gallows fifty cubits high. He stands in the morning air, watching the body swaying in the soft morning breezes while the vultures circle, waiting for their expected prey to be cut down. The workman is transfixed by what he sees. Another worker coming around the corner bumps into him. "Oh, excuse me," he says to the other man. "Who is that?"

"Haven't you heard?" says the first workman. "That's Haman!"

"You mean the king's viceroy, the number-two man in the kingdom?" says the newly arrived workman.

"Yes," he answers. "*They hanged Haman on the gallows he had prepared for Mordecai.*"

Haman is one of the darkest, most sinister characters of Bible lore. Yet there are valuable lessons Christians can learn from Haman's experience about avoiding certain behaviors. The king elevated Haman to be the number-two man in the great Persian Empire, presiding over 127 provinces. Haman answered to no one except King Ahasuerus. Several kingly privileges came to Haman as a result of his promotion. One of Haman's "perks" that was written into his contract required that whenever he appeared in public there would be a blast of trumpets and whoever stood in hearing distance must bow down before Haman as he passed in their midst.

Curiously enough, Haman was not Persian. He originated from the Amalekite nation in the biblical region of Palestine—the congenital enemies of the House of Israel. (There are numerous instances in history where men rise to great power and influence even though they are not indigenous to the land where their influence is felt. For example, Adolf Hitler was not a German; he was Austrian. Stalin was not Russian, but Georgian. Napoleon was not French, but Corsican.)

About the same time Haman secured his new position the annual gathering of the 127 princes took place. Every year King Ahasuerus invited his princes to the capital and all the leaders enjoyed a "knock-down, drag-out party" for seven days! The Bible says, "The king's heart was merry with wine." Translated into contemporary idiom, that means "he was as high as a kite." The princes around the table weren't "feeling any pain either" (if you know what I mean). The king, "into his liquor," began to brag about how "fine" the queen was. One of the princes said, "Oh, nobody could be that fine." So King Ahasuerus ordered one of his seven chamberlains to "go up and bring Queen Vashti down here. Tell her to put on that pink outfit I bought her."

The chamberlain went up and knocked on the door of Vashti's apartment. She came to the door sleepy-eyed, with her hair up in curlers. The servant told her, "The king wants you to come down to the party and you should put on the pink outfit he likes so much."

Vashti looked at her watch and said, "It's three-thirty in the morning. I'm not going anywhere!" She slammed the door.

The chamberlain didn't know what to do. You see, oriental kings do not like hearing bad news. So he went down to the banquet hall and stood there in the doorway shifting from one foot to the other.

The king said, "Well, what is it?"

He answered, "O King live forever, I . . ."

The king said, "What is it?"

He said, "The queen said she's not coming."

Now they tell me that when people are under the influence of alcohol, they presume they're whispering when they're really talking loudly. So the king in his half-drunken stupor yelled, "She'd better come on down here. What does she mean refusing to come when I send for her?"

Two or three nearby princes heard what he shouted. They said, "Uh–oh!" And they started signifying. That's right. They made vicious, negative value judgments, out loud—talking about, "This is bad news. When we get back to our kingdom and we send for our wives, they'll disrespect us. This will never do." They forced the king's hand to take action. He said, "All right, she will no longer be queen of Persia." He banished Vashti in order to keep peace among his princes.

Therefore, the king needed a new queen. Messengers were sent out into all the 127 provinces to find the fairest of the fair. Surprisingly, Esther, who was the second cousin of Mordecai, the spiritual leader of the Jews in captivity, took Vashti's place as queen. When she found out she was going to be the queen, Esther asked her Cousin Mordecai, "Must I tell the king that I am Jewish?"

He said, "No, dear, now is not the time. Just be cool."

It just so happened both of these occurrences ran parallel to each other: the promotion of Haman, this dark evil character, to be the number-two man in the kingdom; and the king's choice of this young Jewish lass, beauteous to look upon, to be his new queen. It is at this juncture that Haman's very existence began to unravel.

Do you remember one of Haman's kingly "perks"? Well, about the third day after his installation, he came out of the palace's main entrance, where the carved lions sat. The first thing he saw was Mordecai the Jew standing ramrod straight.

When the trumpets blasted, everybody bowed down—everybody, that is, except Mordecai. He refused to bow down to Haman because his religion didn't allow him to bow to anyone except the true and the living God.

Haman got into his custom-made carriage and was driven to his elegant home. Haman could have any pomegranate orchard, vineyard, stable of horses, summer or winter home, concubine or wife he chose. But when he entered his home this particular day, his mouth turned down and his face contorted with hatred.

His wife asked, "What is wrong with you?"

He replied, "That blasted Mordecai wouldn't bow down."

Herein is the first lesson discovered from this villainous figure. *You and I need to exercise caution to not let one disappointment in our lives poison our spirits.* We preachers are prone to this! We fix our eye on a certain church, a particular spot on the convention program, or we want to get in the line of apostolic succession, so that one day *we* can be president of the convention. (Hello!) Then someone we weren't even thinking of gets that place of honor and it starts working on our insides.

When the person who was promoted gets up to speak, the signifying in our mind begins. "I've got as much right to be the vice-president as he has." "I've been preaching longer than he has." "He doesn't have a doctorate." "I've written more books than he's written." "He's taking too long with the introduction." "His points didn't hang together." When somebody obtains something you think you ought to have, nothing will ever be right with that person because your spirit has been poisoned. There isn't anything that person can do right. Your stomach is churning, secreting all of those devilish acids, giving you ulcers. And the person doesn't even know you're out there!

This kind of attitude influences folks in the choir, too. (Help me, Holy Ghost!) Some new brothers or sisters come into the fellowship; the Lord has gifted their vocal chords with music, and sanctified them. Next thing you know, the director selects them to lead a song you used to sing. You've been singing it for the last five Easter Sundays! Now, this new member is practicing your song. You make it your business to tell the director, "Huh, she just got here. She has no business singing *my* song. Look at her, she doesn't even know how to walk and she dresses like she's from the country."

People with a negative critical spirit will find everything wrong because the venom of prejudice, envy, and hate is in their system. *You and I have to be careful not to let one disappointment poison our spirits.*

The second lesson Haman teaches Christians is connected to the first. *Once you let the poison of prejudice, envy, and hate get into your life, life becomes a downward spiral.* You decide you'll fix them. You'll get them.

At the close of the first quarter that year, Haman and the king reviewed the faxed reports from the 127 princes. They reviewed the accounts and worked far into the night. At about a quarter to twelve the king began to grow a little weary. Haman suggested that they have a couple of dry martinis to help them unwind.

As they drank, Haman stewed in the juices of his rage. He couldn't get Mordecai off his mind. Haman determined to get him! He had to poison the mind of the king against Mordecai.

He said, "O King live forever, there's something you oughta know, but I just don't want to be the one to tell you."

The king said, "What's that, Haman?"

He said, "There's something you ought to know as king, but I just, I hate to be the one to tell you." Haman held the king's full attention now.

"Well, if it's something I ought to know, Haman, you ought to tell me," the king replied, starting to get a little irritated at Haman's hesitation.

"Well, King Ahasuerus, I just think too much of you, and I don't want to be the one to break it to you. But if you order me to tell you, then I'll have to tell you," Haman replied, sounding as if the king's life depended on this information.

"Well, I order you to tell me!" the king said.

"All right, O King live forever," Haman replied, "if you order me, I'll tell you. Some people live in your empire who don't care anything about you. They have their own traditions and religion. They don't pay any attention to your laws."

"Well," the king asked, "what do you think we ought to do about them?"

Haman reached into his inside pocket and handed the king a memo that he had already prepared: "Post a notice in all of the 127 provinces saying, 'In the month of Adar, on the thirteenth day, every Jew, man-woman-child, shall be slain and all their properties confiscated. I will pay whoever takes care of this business 10,000 talents of silver.'" This notice spelled out a well-defined plan of genocide.

Even in 570 B.C., there was a grapevine in the capital of the Persian Empire.

The maids who overheard the conversation shared the news at breakfast and it hit the neighborhood before lunch. Of course, Mordecai found out. Bright and early the next morning Mordecai was in the king's courtyard dressed in sackcloth and ashes. That was a no-no. Oriental kings do not like bad news. Sackcloth and ashes telegraph the fact that there is bad news abroad in the land.

It also got around to Queen Esther's quarters that someone was in the king's courtyard moaning and groaning. The queen inquired, "Who is out there making all that racket?"

Someone replied, "That's your cousin, Mordecai."

She said, "Find out what the problem is."

In response, Mordecai sent word to Esther and said: "Darling, you remember that when you became queen, I told you be cool, wait a while, and not tell the king that you're a Jew. Now the time has come for you to tell him. You need to go to the king to save your people."

By now, the queen's new lifestyle fit her quite well. She slid back the doors of her walk-in closet and allowed her eyes to caress the Yves St. Laurent and Balenciaga gowns hanging there. She went over to the picture window, looked out, and there was her cream-colored Lincoln Continental with the rag top, parked next to her 560 Mercedes Benz SEL, sitting next to her Silver Cloud Rolls Royce. Queen Esther was wondering why she was being called upon to jeopardize all of this in order to save her people.

While Esther was doing all of this musing, Mordecai's patience ran out. He sent word to her: "Listen, girl; let me tell you something. If you can't make up your mind soon enough, God won't need you; he'll find another way to save his people." This sharp response from Mordecai straightened Queen Esther right up. That's when she coined that marvelous phrase, "If I perish, I perish. I'm going to see the king."

Let me take a little detour here. You can get dissatisfied and upset in your church-family and begin to talk about what you "ain't gonna do no more," because someone bent you out of shape. "I ain't gonna Deac' no more." "I ain't gonna Trustee no more." "I ain't gonna sing no more." Because someone bent you out of shape! *You have to be careful talking about what you ain't gonna do no more, because you don't know how much "no more" you got left!*

No one sashayed into the king's presence on their own accord. Anyone who presented themselves before an oriental monarch without being summoned risked the threat of immediate death. When you knelt before the king uninvited, he either touched your shoulder gently with the scepter—his authority symbol—indicating that it's okay for you to be in his presence or he instantly had you assassinated.

The late great Dr. Vernon Johns (predecessor to Dr. Martin Luther King at the Dexter Avenue Baptist Church in Montgomery, Alabama) had a uniquely descriptive way of ushering Queen Esther into that throne room—he says, "The beauteous Queen Esther stepped into the throne room, a shimmering gown clinging to her lithe body. Every step was a symphony of motion. A precious jewel hanging about her neck caught a straggling ray of daylight and threw it back in defiance at the sun."

When Esther knelt before the king, he took his scepter and broke it across his knee and said, "Baby, tell me what you want."

She said, "O King live forever, If I have found favor in thy sight, I have a request of thee."

He said, "What is it, darling? Looking as good as you look, you can get up to half of the kingdom." (She must have been looking good!)

Queen Esther said, "What I would like to do is have a little wine and cheese banquet this afternoon, when you finish with your desk work—just you, me, and Haman."

The king replied, "Is that all you want, Darling?"

Esther answered, "Yes, that's all I want for right now."

"No problem," Ahasuerus replied.

About half an hour later, Haman came skipping in and the king said to him, "Haman, I have some good news for you."

Haman said, "What's that, O King live forever?"

King Ahasuerus said, "Queen Esther's never given a banquet for anyone before. She wants to have a little wine and cheese with you and me. Can you make it at five ... say about five-thirty?"

Haman, out of his mind with delight, replied, "Oh yes, of course, I would be honored." (He was just ripe and ready.)

At 5:30 this private little evening party settled in with a banquet of wine and cheese. King Ahasuerus said, "Uh, now, Darling, you're still looking good. You know I'm kinda getting up in age and I can't stand much teasing by someone as young and fine as you. Come on," he said, "tell me what it is you really want."

Queen Esther said, "O King live forever, if I've found favor in your sight, what I'd like to do is have a full banquet supper tomorrow night and then I'll tell you what's really on my mind."

The king asked, "Well, who's gonna be at this banquet?"

She said, "Just you, me, and Haman."

Well, Lord have mercy! Haman left the room floating on a cloud. Up to this time, no one had obtained an audience with the new queen. First, she invited him to a small banquet of wine and cheese and now to a full banquet with all the trimmings with no one but the king, queen, and himself. He couldn't wait to get home to tell his wife, Zeresh. He bounded out of the door and the first thing that greeted his eye was Mordecai mourning in sackcloth and ashes.

The trumpets blasted for Haman and everybody bowed down except Mordecai, who stood up ramrod straight!

Haman got into his coach and went home. When he got home he broke the news. "Zeresh," Haman said to his wife, "guess what?"

Zeresh said, "What?"

He said, "I had . . . I had a . . . a wine-and-cheese banquet with the new queen."

She said, "Go 'way!"

He said, "Yeah. And let me tell you something else."

She said, "Now what?"

Haman said, "Tomorrow night she's giving a full-blown banquet, and there won't be anybody there but the king, queen, and me."

"Oh, that's so nice," Zeresh said, "but why is your face so all bent out of shape?"

He said, "When I came out of the palace today, that blasted Mordecai didn't bow down."

"I'm sick and tired of hearing you talk about this Mordecai," Zeresh responded. "If I were you, I would build a gallows fifty cubits high and hang that rascal on it."

Haman's face lit up. "That is exactly what I'll do," he said.

He picked up the phone, called the Artisans' Headquarters, and ordered them to build a gallows on the west side of the palace—over there in front of Haman's office. Now he could be rid of this troublesome Jew once and for all.

Living in Hell

Then he could attend the banquet tomorrow night with nary a care on his mind.

If you look closely at the book of Esther (where God's name is never mentioned), you will find a curious verse at the beginning of the sixth chapter. It says, "On that night the king could not sleep."

On *that* night!
Not the night before,
Not the next night,
Not three nights earlier,
Not three nights later,
Not a week earlier,
Not a week later,
Not a month earlier or later,
But on *that* night the king could not sleep!

On the one side of the palace that housed Haman's administrative quarters, the carpenters were building a gallows—fifty cubits high. On the other side of the palace, on *that* night, the king could not sleep.

King Ahasuerus said to his chamberlain, "Go get the Chronicles and read me a passage, maybe that will ease my insomnia."

So the chamberlain began reading, "Mmmm, mmmm, mmmm . . . in the year . . . and in the month of . . . and then, and then, oh yes, Bigthana and Teresh, two conspirators, made a plan to assassinate the king . . . but it was revealed through Mordecai the Jew about the plan, and the king was . . ."

The king said, "Wait a minute. Read that again."

Again, the chamberlain read about Mordecai the Jew being instrumental in foiling a plot by Bigthana and Teresh to kill the king. Astonished, the king asked, "Was this Mordecai the Jew ever rewarded?"

The chamberlain said, "Let me check the footnotes. Hmm, I don't see any record of a reward."

The king said, "That's fine. I'm all right now. You may go." And the king went to sleep.

Haman's plan was in place. Bright and early the next morning he saw that the gallows stood fifty cubits high on the west side of the palace, near his executive suite. Today was the day he would have a full-fledged banquet with the king and queen. Haman had outdone himself. He raced over to the throne room to share his plans and happiness with the king.

As he entered he said, "O King live forever, guess what?"

King Ahasuerus said, "Just a minute." And when the king says, just a minute, everything stops. "Haman, you have a fertile mind. What would you suggest I do unto him whom the king delighteth to honor?"

Well, gee whiz, Haman thought, who else would the king want to honor but the number-two man in the kingdom? The wheels of his mind began to race. He said, "I'll tell you what I would do, O King live forever. I would have the chamberlains get out the Royal Stallion, have it decked out in the Royal Livery, place the Royal Crown on your honoree's head, get the most important Prince of the nation to go through the streets leading that animal and cry out all over town, 'Unto him whom the king delighteth to honor!'"

The king said, "That's exactly what I want you to do. Make haste! Get it all done. Mordecai is the man I want to honor!"

Can't you just picture Haman? He deeply hated the Jews in general and Mordecai in particular. He strolled reluctantly down Broadway in Shushan, the capital of the Persian Empire, carrying the cord to a Royal Stallion draped in the Royal Livery. Mordecai was seated on the king's horse with the Royal Crown on his head while Haman led the horse and walked beside him—crying out, "Unto him whom the king delighteth to honor!"

When the parade ended, Haman crept back to his house and told his wife, "It's all over."

"What's wrong?" Zeresh asked him. Haman reported the events of the day.

She said, "Well, you can't leave town."

He said, "I've got to leave town."

She said, "But the king's limousine is waiting to take you to this banquet you've been telling me about!"

Haman slipped into his tuxedo, got into the king's limousine, and went to the banquet. Then he was with the king and queen. The king was a little nettled by now. Here he wasn't a young man anymore, and he could not bear not knowing what his fine, statuesque queen wanted. He said, "Come on, Darling, you just have to tell me. I'm about to bust wide open with curiosity. Tell me what you want."

Esther said, "O King live forever, I should have told you earlier. I am a Jew. My people are the victims of a genocide plot orchestrated by one of your high-ranking officials."

The king said, "Who . . . who . . . who would do that?"

She said, "Haman."

The king was so angry that he rushed out into the garden. Haman, knowing his life dangled on the line, ran over and flopped down next to Queen Esther—falling into her lap. (In those days, people reclined on pillows at low tables in order to eat.) When the king walked back into the room, that is the scene that greeted him. Haman's on the queen's lap! The king shouted, "You mean to tell me you will assault my wife in my presence?" Someone tore a tapestry from the wall and put it over Haman's face, "the death veil," so the king wouldn't have to look at him.

King Ahasuerus said, "I . . . I'm so angry that I . . . I don't know what to do with him."

Harbonah, one of the chamberlains, spoke up and said, "There's a gallows fifty cubits high on the west side of the palace. Hang Haman on it!" So they hanged Haman on the gallows that he had prepared for Mordecai.

We had a Haman in our midst not long ago. (Now, you thought that this was a nice little Bible story with its faraway drama, but it is today's headline.) His name is George Herbert Walker Bush. Do you remember how he got to the presidency?

By parading the picture of Willie Horton all over the country—scaring white folks in a nervous democracy into believing that "this might happen to your daughter if these black folks get their person in." He was making a caricature of a black mother's son gone wrong. Then, less than a year later, George Herbert Walker Bush's son, Neal, was found to be all mixed up in the savings and loan mess. *You should be very careful about who you try to hang.*

As you go down life's pathway and something goes wrong in your life or someone possesses something you think you ought to have, keep these things in mind: First of all, don't get bent out of shape about how God blesses other people. This world is big enough for you, him and her. You ought to be grateful. While God blessed you, he also found time to go and bless someone else.

Second, remember that Jesus instructs us to "Love your enemies. Bless them that curse you. Do good to them that hate you. Pray for them which despitefully use you and persecute you, for great is your reward in heaven."

If you continue to experience a difficult time accepting the hard challenges in your life and are filled with envy of others, flip the switch on the magnificent television of your sanctified imagination. Find yourself at the junction of the Tigris and Euphrates rivers in Shushan, Babylonia, in 570 B.C. at ten minutes to six in the morning. Inhale the fragrance of jasmine and narcissus in the heavy, moist, early-morning air. Turn that corner in the capital of the Persian Empire, where the carved lions sit, and catch in your peripheral vision the sight of a body hanging from a gallows fifty cubits high. Watch as vultures circle 'round waiting for their prey to be cut down. You will be confronted again with the fact that Haman was hung on the gallows he had prepared for Mordecai. *Be careful who you try to hang!* ✞

How to Get Out of Hell

Psalm 16:10−11; 137:1−6

Alfred D. Hill (B.A., American Baptist Seminary; D.Min., Louisville Presbyterian Theological Seminary) is pastor of the Pilgrim Rest Baptist Church in Memphis, Tennessee.

How to Get Out of Hell

For thou wilt not leave my soul in hell; neither wilt thou suffer thine Holy One to see corruption. Thou wilt show me the path of life; in thy presence is fulness of joy; at thy right hand there are pleasures for evermore.... By the rivers of Babylon, there we sat down, yea, we wept, when we remembered Zion. We hanged our harps upon the willows in the midst thereof. For there they that carried us away captive required of us a song; and they that wasted us required of us mirth, saying, Sing us one of the songs of Zion. How shall we sing the Lord's song in a strange land? If I forget thee, O Jerusalem, let my right hand forget her cunning. If I do not remember thee, let my tongue cleave to the roof of my mouth; if I prefer not Jerusalem above my chief joy (PSALM 16:10–11; 137:1–6 KJV).

In his book *Whatever Became of Sin?* psychiatrist Karl Menninger seeks to identify the relationship between mental and moral health. The quest of this respected and reputable voice in the field of psychiatry is allied with our own because the subject of sin raises the issue of hell. Menninger believes that "the word 'sin' has almost disappeared from our vocabulary, but the sense of guilt remains in our hearts and minds."[1]

Like Dr. Menninger I am inquiring about another term no longer commonly used. What happened to the word "hell"? (With the possible exception of those wishing to consign and send persons to hell, the word has almost disappeared.) At one time, the subject of hell was prominent, as seen in the theme of

Dante's famous *Paradise Lost*; it was pivotal in John Bunyan's *Pilgrim's Progress*. Jonathan Edwards, who belonged to the era of American Christianity known as the "Great Awakening," once preached an explosive, fiery sermon entitled "Sinners in the Hands of an Angry God." Edwards characterized men as spiders being held by fragile webs over the burning, blistering, and boiling flames of an eternal hell. Yet, despite the absence of the term "hell," evidence of its reality remains in our times.

How do we get out of hell? Such was the concern of an ancient Psalmist. He announced this concern in a hymn of deep trust and confidence. In the Psalm he expressed the stubborn belief that there is a means of escape for those who are prisoners of hell. It is not God's will to allow hell to be the final arbiter for his children: "For thou wilt not leave my soul in hell; neither wilt thou suffer thine Holy One to see corruption" (Psalm 16:10 KJV).

EXILES IN A STRANGE LAND

What do we mean by hell? For some it is everlasting torment, a place of weeping, wailing, and gnashing of teeth. It has also been called the place of eternal darkness. For others, hell is the destination of wicked and unrepentant sinners. Evangelicals call hell "the imprisonment and destruction of the soul";[2] the second death; the final judgment for every man, woman, boy or girl who continues to say "No!" to Jesus' invitation to allow him entrance into their lives.

Paul Tillich called hell "complete separation from eternity."[3] This is the implication of Jesus' well-known parable concerning the rich man who died and went to hell and the poor man who went to Abraham's bosom (Luke 16:19–31). "And in hell he lift up his eyes, being in torments, and seeth Abraham afar off, and Lazarus in his bosom" (v. 23 KJV). The rich man desired a cool drink of water to quench his dry, parched throat amid the scalding, sizzling, sweltering heat of a burning hell. But the rich man's request was denied. It could not be granted because he had refused to give a small morsel of bread from his table to this poor man. Consequently, a great gulf divided the two. The poor man was in Abraham's bosom, while the rich man suffered in hell. They were eternally independent and detached from each other. Before death they could have touched each other in many ways, but now neither can reach the other because in death sin has claimed one and righteousness the other.

Such was the situation of Judah in Babylonian exile. She was a nation severed from her native land. The prophet Ezekiel was moved to write, "Behold, they say, Our bones are dried, and our hope is lost: we are cut off for our parts" (Ezekiel 37:11 KJV). In Babylon, down by the river called Chebar, the people of Judah experienced a living hell.

Presently, millions of African-Americans are forced to live the same way. This is our history. We were separated from the land of our fathers and cut off from the country of our roots, like a branch from a tree and a root out of dry ground. Africans who survived the dehumanizing, degrading, grotesque "middle passage" on slave ships made it to America to live a "cutoff" lifestyle. For over 300 years African-Americans have been forced to live a disjointed, dissected, disconnected, disunited, living, breathing, airtight hell of an existence.

Walk up and down the streets of America's urban ghettos and listen to the cries of African-Americans. There is pathos in our lamentations. One can hear the mournful sighs of the elderly, the homeless, and the unemployed. Agony, sorrow, and pain resound in our conversations. This is not senseless wordiness, but the distressed outcry of a people cut off from power and full participation in this land. People of color in this country are politically hindered from determining their own destinies; they continually struggle with unemployment, police brutality, inadequate health care, political dishonesty, black-on-black crime, poorly funded educational systems, and more. This is hell!

THE SONG OF THE OPPRESSED

The celebration of that which is unique to an oppressed people is crucial to their adjustment to a life in hell. But entertainment required by captors is not the same as celebration by captives. Such is evident in the desire of those who held Judah captive in Babylon. "Sing for us," the captors demanded, "one of the songs of Zion." Sing us one of *your* songs! These were Judah's hymns. Their lyrics were not composed amid the sweltering flames of Babylonian confinement. Judah brought them with her, the products of her people's minds and souls! Judah sang when Babylon invaded their camps, and laid them waste, in what Ezekiel described as "a valley . . . full of dry bones" (Ezekiel 37:1).

Dr. Fred C. Lofton (pastor of the Metropolitan Baptist Church of Memphis and past president of the Progressive National Baptist Convention) said that God has given to the oppressed gifts, which he has not given to the oppressor. These gifts are reflected in how hell's citizens do certain things. For African-Americans the gift reveals itself in music—spirituals, gospel songs, blues, and jazz. Our patterns and rhythm is also evident in poetry, dance, and even in our gathered experiences of worship.

"Sing us one of the songs of Zion." To do so in exile is to rehearse an oppressed people's worldview. Judah's hymns were more than rhythm and rhyme. They were the collective expressions of how God's chosen people viewed the landscape. Who can review the Psalms, the great hymn tradition of Israel, and not conclude that this is a people's way of looking at life? To sing those hymns is to continue that celebration of their worldview.

That is what African-Americans do when we celebrate what is unique to us. Inside the experience of African-American religion is what William B. McClain called "geniusness."[4] It is this which has sustained and brought African-Americans through personal Egypts, Red Seas, wildernesses, and even Gethsemanes. It is celebration which affirms life. C. Eric Lincoln, author of *The*

Black Experience in Religion, says, "It reflects a life style of persons living on the existential edge where the creative and the destructive, the wise and the foolish, the sacred and the secular, the agony and the ecstasy, the ups and the downs, are the contrarieties of human existence in the presence of the divine."[5]

THE POWER OF A MIND SET FREE

Finally, when a people celebrate they discover a door of escape for the mind through the maintenance of a sense of history. At several points in our experience this fact thunders through to us. One of them is in the words of Richard Lovelace, a Dutchman who was born to an old Kentish family in 1618. In 1642 Lovelace found himself imprisoned for presenting a petition to the hostile House of Commons, in the Gatehouse of Old London. From his prison cell, he wrote to one named Althea:

> Stone walls do not a prison make,
> Nor iron bars a cage;
> Minds innocent and quiet take
> That for a hermitage;
> If I have freedom in my love,
> And in my soul am free,
> Angels alone that soar above
> Enjoy such liberty.[6]

How does the African-American mind and soul trapped behind the iron bars of a living hell find a way to transcend entrapment while the body is not free? Can the mind and soul wing its way up and beyond to regions of pure delight while restricted at the same time? Judah knew this possibility amid the horrors of exile. She expressed it in the gift of memory: "If I forget thee, O Jerusalem, let my right hand forget her cunning. If I do not remember thee, let my tongue cleave to the roof of my mouth; if I prefer not Jerusalem above my chief joy." Judah sought to hold on to her roots, for her history made her—the chosen people of God. Although living in Babylon, Babylon did not make her—and Babylon was not in her. The essence of Judah remained united with Jerusalem. How could she forget Zion? Her homeland was more than a place—Zion was her history.

It is always an invitation to tragedy when people forget their roots. To be held captive is devastating enough, but forgetting one's past only intensifies the living hell. To measure identity and ability by the standards of the people who confine them is tragic. This is the misfortune of adopting the lifestyles, models, thoughts, and attitudes of one's captors. We add continuity to our imprisonment. Those sun-burnt, ebony children of long ago understood this very well.

Standing tall among the trees of African-American history is Reverend C. T. Walker, revered for his unique mastery of the pulpit and known to thousands as "the black Spurgeon." In 1888, Walker preached the centennial sermon for the black Baptists of Georgia, who met in Forest City. Reverend Walker said, "Young men have come to get inspiration from a review of the work of the Fathers and to return to their churches electrified and encouraged . . ."[7] Walker knew, like Judah, that there is a creative and invigorating power in the ability to recall the events of yesterday. That power sets the mind free and fulfills the assurance of the Psalmist, "Thou wilt not leave my soul in hell."

The life of the carpenter of Nazareth echoes this one central fact—that African-Americans can be free from hell while living in the midst of hell.

> Jesus, born into our hell—into a world,
> splintered, divided, broken, and corrupt.
> This world laid hold on his body,
> Plotful hands betrayed it,
> Vicious hands arrested it,
> Callous hands beat it,
> Insensitive hands broke its flesh.
> But Jesus lived outside of the cruelties
> Fired by hatred, resentments, and ugliness.
> When the world proved cruel,
> Jesus was kind.

When it hated,
He practiced an unending,
Never dying, creative and redemptive love.
When that world alienated itself from the poor,
Jesus drew them to himself with cords of compassion.
When the world identified
The disfigured, repellent, and repugnant in man,
Jesus saw what was beautiful,
Embellished, elegant and sublime.
It is no mystery Jesus could say of his life before Calvary,
"No man taketh it from me, but I lay it down of myself"
    (John 10:18 KJV).

Jesus' soul, mind, and spirit were not confined to this hellish world he entered as a baby. Jesus took "The Old Rugged Cross"— "an emblem of suffering and shame"—and exchanged it for a crown to be worn by the faithful, the twice-born sons and daughters of redemption who have mastered the art of being free from hell. ✠

Notes

1. Karl Menninger, *Whatever Became of Sin?* (New York: Hawthorn Books, 1973), 1.

2. Donald Bloesch, *Essentials of Evangelical Theology: God, Authority and Salvation* (San Francisco: Harper & Row, 1982).

3. Paul Tillich, *Systematic Theology,* vol. 1 (Chicago: University of Chicago Press, 1951), 284.

4. William B. McClain, "The Genius of the Black Church," *Christianity and Crisis* 30 (November 2, 1970): 250.

5. C. Eric Lincoln, *The Black Experience in Religion* (New York: Doublday Anchor, 1973), 4.

6. John Bartlett, *Familiar Quotations* (Boston: Little, Brown, 1968), 358f.

7. C. T. Walker, unpublished sermon.

Have Your Own

Proverbs 5:15

Randolph Meade Walker (B.A., Hampton University; M.A., University of Memphis; Ph.D., Memphis State University) is pastor of the New Philadelphia Baptist Church in Memphis, Tennessee.

Have Your Own

Drink waters out of thine own cistern, and running waters out of thine own well (PROVERBS 5:15 KJV).

This passage is an allegory, specifically referring to fidelity in marriage. No one should covet another's spouse. One of the commandments of the Decalogue prohibits such unethical and unrighteous behavior (Exodus 20:14).

Despite the merits of this singular application of the Scripture to marriage, it also has a wider practicality. This is especially true for the peculiar historical struggle of the African-American. With the advice of this Scripture as a guiding light, let us explore where the African-American has been, where he is now, and where he needs to go.

In the not too distant past, many African-Americans abandoned the development of their own institutions. During the quest for civil rights, African-Americans rushed to integrate white institutions.[1] In the euphoria of being accepted by mainstream America, many people of color left their neighborhoods in favor of previously lily-white enclaves. The crossover of black consumers to previously "white-only" establishments contributed to the failure of African-American owned businesses. A result was the loss of jobs. Thus, ironically, the winning of civil rights helped African-Americans lose enthusiasm for their own institutional development.

In their desire to be received by the wider society, the African-Americans failed to build anything for themselves. Consequently, the African-American man became a beggar. He applied for admission to white schools, he asked for jobs whites created and controlled, he sought housing in white neighborhoods, he desired membership in white country clubs, and in some instances, he even asked for admission to "white-only" churches.

The unbalanced tragedy of this trend is that whites did not reciprocate. Caucasians did not integrate African-American institutions. They automatically assumed the black schools, churches, and businesses ranked inferior to their white counterparts. Sadly, many African-American people accepted the European-American assumptions about black institutional inferiority. Therefore, African-American students swelled the enrollment on white campuses. Alumni of historically black colleges sent their sons and daughters to the larger white schools. Likewise, African-American people quit eating at black-owned cafes, and instead patronized white-owned restaurants. In some rare instances, African-Americans even procured an European-American mortuary to bury their dead.

This rush toward patronizing and supporting white establishments is demonstrative of the psychological hell in which people of color live. The deplorable element in this kind of oppression is that the oppressed do not realize they are exploited. African-Americans have accepted the indoctrination that everything European is proper. They operate like a people without the power of choice. Psychologically, they are captives. The African-American is so mentally shackled that he cannot choose to support his own race's endeavors. The enslaved thinking tells him that African-American people cannot do anything that is comparable in quality to that of the European. Thus, a psychological hell drives the African-American away from a black-owned business or institution to "crawl" to the white-controlled business or institution.

What has this mad rush to integrate white institutions gotten the African-American? In terms of white perceptions, it has gotten him the reputation of an intruder. He is viewed as a beggar who has nothing of his own and therefore wishes to encroach upon others' facilities. The African-American is regarded as being an aggressive panhandler, correct or not. White America views the African-American as an unwelcome, overly pushy nuisance.

The African-American is viewed as a pauper wanting another's well or cistern. For example, shortly after the passage of the Civil Rights Bill of 1964, an article appeared in *Parents' Magazine* entitled "The First Negro Family on Maple Terrace." The first white family interviewed about the prospects of a black neighbor gave the following response: "I'm against niggers on this block. I wouldn't want to see a bunch of little spades playing with my kids, and big black bucks strutting up and down the street. And no black woman comes into my house except through the back door to do the laundry. The day a nigger family moves to Maple Terrace, the Heaths move out."[2]

This obviously racist comment is not cited as being representative of even a majority of white Americans. Yet, it does sound the alarm of a widespread fear of the black intruder. For example, a more moderate response from another neighbor on Maple Terrace was, "When we consider the possibility of a Negro family moving in down the block, we pause. And into this pause rush the pictures, emotions, thoughts, and prejudices we connect with the word 'Negro.'"[3] Thus, the prospect of desegregation is seen as a threat, from both the vocal racist and the moderate. The African-American was not welcome to the white man's cistern or well.

Consequently, the African-American race is not respected. Beggars are not highly regarded. They are seen as parasites who look for a host to attach themselves. Black people are characterized as leeches, chinches, or ticks. Such deadbeats do not contribute to others. They only draw blood from their victims for their own consumption.

It is easy to see why such a perception results in a lack of respect for African-American men. Everyone loathes a bum. Questions are instantly raised when one is confronted on the streets by a panhandler. Why is the beggar not working? Why can't he support himself? What is it that he needs? What is he going to do with what he receives? Why does he not receive some kind of government support?

Needless to say, no clear-thinking parent wants to see a child locked into a career of panhandling. No responsible father wants to give his daughter in matrimony to an unemployed groom who lacks prospects for economic productivity. Such a destitute person is not welcome in a family that has drive and potential.

Unfortunately, as a race of people, African-Americans are generally not helping themselves economically, nor engaging in self-help, but looking for others to do for them what they should be doing for themselves. For example, African-Americans depend upon others to provide jobs for their people, while cursing white conservative Christians for lack of social concern. We then admitted as patients to hospitals founded and supported by those same Fundamentalists!

Generally, African-American people are not as vigilant about finances as they should be. They need to be conserving and investing their resources. Consequently, they are dependent consumers who lack power to control the means of production. African-Americans have the potential to be influential in this area, but they do not tap their potential.

For example, at this present time, the African-American is virtually landless. As the race became more urbanized during the twentieth century, black real-estate ownership shrank drastically. In 1987, African-Americans occupied and owned 4,458,000 housing units, while living in 5,794,000 rental units.[4]

In comparison, the total American population owns 58,164,000 units, while renting only 32,724,000 units.[5] The message here is clear. The African-American lives in more than a million more rental units than he owns. On the other hand, the total American population at large owns more than 25 million more units than are rented! Is it not time someone told the African-American to possess his own cistern?

During the same period that the African-American man held so little real estate, 1,729,000 black households drove more than two cars.[6] Sad to say, but these figures still confirm the validity of Dr. Vernon Johns' definition of perpetual motion as "The average Negro trying to park his Cadillac on some land he owns."[7]

Further misuse of resources can be seen in the African-American purchases of wasteful materials. In 1987, while African-Americans composed approximately 10–12 percent of the American population, black people twenty years and older purchased 33.5 percent of the cigarettes sold.[8] Needless to say, this literally burns up money that could otherwise be spent on investments that would appreciate in value.

According to a 1985 survey, 29.3 percent of all African-Americans sixteen years of age and older ingested five or more alcoholic drinks on any given day the previous year.[9] While this was less than the 38.3 percent figure for whites, it is a waste that African-Americans cannot afford. This is acutely the case because the African-American owns few reserves and assets. As long as the black race remains in such a vulnerable position, it must be understood that we cannot afford to imitate the squandering habits of others who already own their own cisterns.

Again, we see the manifestation of psychological exploitation. The African-American community's misuse of its resources is at least attributable to the white-controlled, capitalist marketing system. A constant parade of advertisements displays a stream of products before black audiences for their consumption. Black-oriented media readily obtain advertising for cigarettes, alcohol, and automobiles. On the other hand, advertisements that send a message for investment in stocks, mutual funds and real estate are virtually nonexistent in the same media. As a result, the African-American listening to ethnically attractive radio stations and reading black newspapers or magazines is mentally conditioned to be only a consumer and not an investor.

The only way the African-American man will reverse his impoverished, dependent status is to change his self-perception. He must view himself as capable. He must open his eyes to what

God's already done for him and believe in himself by believing in God. He must appreciate the fact that the Almighty made him in his divine image. God made African-Americans just like he made everyone else. People of African descent normally have two eyes, two ears, two legs, and two hands just like all other people.

The African-American needs to quit majoring in negative thought. He must retire from focusing upon what's missing and what we are unable to do. Some African-Americans are like the Old Testament Jews when they first prepared to enter the Promised Land. They saw themselves as grasshoppers in a land of giants (Numbers 13:31–33). To them the obstacles outweighed the opportunities. As an institution of faith, however, the African-American church must declare to the masses that if God be for us, there is no opposition of consequence (Romans 8:31). The African-American Christian must realize that through Christ Jesus we can do all things (Philippians 4:13). The African-American community must be taught that with God nothing is impossible (Luke 1:37).

> God is able to speak worlds into existence (Genesis 1:14).
> God is able to separate land from water (Genesis 1:9).
> God is able to scoop valleys out of the earth's floor.
> God is able to make mountains bulge up above sea level,
>   then to clothe their bony shoulders with fleecy white
>   clouds.
> God is able to carpet the landscape with green grass,
>   then in the early morning hours
>   he places diamond-like dewdrops upon every blade of
>   grass.
> God causes the rose to blush red in the spring of the year.
> The Almighty acts as a conductor of nature's symphony
>   by signaling the sparrow to chirp
>   and the whippoorwill to repeat the chorus.
> Indeed, God is a great God!
> With him all things are possible.
> He is able to take nobodies and make them somebodies.
> He can turn cursers into blessers.

He specializes in elevating the downtrodden.
He turned shepherd boys into kings.
He turned persecutors into preachers.
He turned slaves into liberators.
He turned sinners into saints.

If only one African-American can believe on the Lord Jesus Christ, who came into a rebellious world for the remission of sins, he can be made whole. This wholeness also involves enabling individuals to own wells and cisterns. When we turn our lives over to Jesus, we can be respected and accepted at the welcome table of brotherhood. Jesus will bring us honor here and now as well as in the world to come. ✢

Notes

1. *Tri-State Defender*, April 5, 1990; September 15, 1990.
2. *Parents' Magazine and Better Homemaking* 15 (January 1965).
3. Ibid.
4. Bureau of the Census, *Statistical Abstract of the United States, 1990* (Washington, D.C.: 1990), 724.
5. Ibid.
6. Ibid.
7. Taylor Branch, *Parting the Waters: America in the King Years, 1954–63* (New York: Simon & Schuster, 1988), 16.
8. Bureau of the Census, 123.
9. Ibid., 122.

Part II

SERMONS
From the
NEW
TESTAMENT

The Church as a Healing Agent:
Let the Church Be the Church
Matthew 5:13

Douglas I. Miles (B.A., Johns Hopkins University;

M.A., St. Mary's Seminary & University; D.D.,Virginia

Seminary & College) is pastor of the Koinonia Baptist

Church in Baltimore, Maryland.

The Church as a Healing Agent: Let the Church Be the Church

Ye are the salt of the earth: but if the salt have lost his savour, wherewith shall it be salted? It is thenceforth good for nothing, but to be cast out, and to be trodden under foot of men (MATTHEW 5:13 KJV).

The facts and figures of the dilemma we face in the African-American community are staggering. The statistical evidence—escalating teen pregnancy rates, rapidly increasing incarceration rates for African-American males, the drug epidemic, black male murder rates—all paint a graphic picture of our plight. Many programs have been designed in response to these alarming conditions. But rather than follow up with more facts and figures or suggest other programmatic approaches to the problem, I want to reflect on a few recent events in my own experience that I believe sum up the breadth of the problem. Also, I will take a look at what I believe to be God's call to African-American Christians in these troubled times.

Some time ago, on a pleasant spring day, I walked home from church. I was accosted by a group of African-American youth, between the ages of twelve and fifteen. One boy held a hunting knife and another, the group leader, revealed a small-caliber handgun. The head of the group, a boy of fourteen, demanded money from me along with the few pieces of jewelry I usually wear. When I refused, he pointed the gun at me and pulled the trigger. The gun misfired. Thanks be to God, I escaped with my life—unscathed physically but shaken emotionally. The police apprehended the young men. After the investigation, I found out that not one of those boys belonged to a church. Most of the boys came from fragmented homes and not one of them was an achiever in school.

I sat in a District Youth Fellowship worship service that was led by a capable young man serving as district president of the Christian Youth Fellowship. What a time we had—singing, praying, and praising God. Before the week ended, police arrested the young man that had led the worship service (he was implicated in a shooting incident which resulted in the death of another youth). This was a young person from a stable home environment, doing well in school, and he attended church every Sunday.

Recently, I picked up my sixteen-year-old son from school. When he got into the car, his face showed obvious distress. My son described to me the turmoil that exists both at school and on the school bus. The conversation ended with a dire prediction by my son—that by the year 2010, not one African-American will be left in America. Here is a young man whose father is a preacher, who is an active participant in the church—one who has demonstrated at his young age a distinct love for the Lord and a commitment to treating others right—yet my son feels hopeless about his future and powerless to change the deteriorating situation around him.

Each of these incidents brought its own level of uneasiness and pain. Individually and in combination these situations have haunted me and forced me into agonizing soul-searching, situation-specific prayer, and painstaking inquiry. These incidents raise serious questions.

With all the churches in the African-American community, why are we being torn asunder on such an epic scale? With the numerous preachers, Sunday school teachers, missionaries, deacons (stewards), choir members, ushers, and special programs, why has the quality of and reverence for life among us dropped so low? How can the church bring healing to a community that is drowning in violence and overwhelmed by anger and despair?

I have discovered that it is dangerous to raise such questions to the Lord because he has been known to give answers that are not always pleasant to hear. The Lord responded, "Ye are the salt of the earth: but if the salt have lost his savour, wherewith shall it be salted?" (Matthew 5:13).

I believe that if we hear Jesus' words anew and allow the Spirit to speak to us, the Lord will reveal to us as least three insights and instruct us in ways the church can be a healing agent. I believe that in these insights God is saying to believers, "Let the church be the church."

ON BEING DIFFERENT

As the salt of the earth, we Christians are called to be noted by our purity and by our difference from those around us.

Truthfully, there is not much difference today between professing Christians and unbelievers having no allegiance to him. As a pastor, I have baptized or dedicated children born out of wedlock to members of the church. I have visited church members and/or their children in jail. I have presided at the funerals of members murdered in one way or another. I counsel church members strung out on drugs. And I am aware of church folk who either buy or sell "hot goods." I have witnessed just as much divisiveness in churches and our denominations as evidenced among warring political factions in the community. I witness every day the attitude of greed among Christians who say, "I've got mine; you've got yours to get." This kind of mind set rules American economic life.

But I hear Jesus saying, "Ye are the salt of the earth. ..." Christians are called to be unique—not better—but different. One reason there is so little difference between believers and the secular world is because too much of our time and effort is devoted to "church work" and not enough to "the work of the church."

Juan Carlos Ortiz, in his marvelous little book *Disciple*, tells of the rude awakening he had concerning what the church ought to be about. Despite unusual success in ministry, Ortiz grew tentative about his direction. He was uneasy despite the church's increased membership, and he was frustrated by what he perceived to be the lack of significant lifestyle change in the membership. Ortiz took some time away from the ministry to devote to prayer and meditation. He wanted clear direction from the Lord as to what he was doing wrong. In his search he heard the Lord speak:

> Juan Carlos, where is my finger in all this? You are dealing with my things—and you are promoting them as Coca-Cola promotes its products, as *Reader's Digest* sells records and books. You are not growing, you are just getting fat. You just have more people of the same kind. You had 200 without love ... and now 600 all without love. More of the same ... not growing ... getting fat. Yours is not a church; it is an orphanage. No one there has a parent; all are orphans and you are the director of an orphanage. Sundays, you fill a bottle of milk and say, "Now open your mouth." And you think you are feeding your people.

What the Lord said to Juan Ortiz he could very well say to the leaders of most churches which are not growing, maturing, changing folk, or impacting communities for the better, but just getting fat. When we stop to think about it, it really doesn't take much to be a church member. If one gives a little money, attends services often, and is not openly a heretic, a person can stay on the church roll from the time of baptism until he or she is called home to glory. There are no demands made upon members to be priestly in their service, prophetic in their living, or passionate in their proclamation. Therefore, when folk are not challenged to grow up in their faith, we end up with

- Worship that's more entertaining than uplifting
- Trustees who can't be trusted
- Missionaries with no mission

- Stingy stewards
- Uncommitted choir members
- Dishonest deacons
- Picky pew sitters
- Unruly ushers
- And pimping preachers

All too often preachers and pastors get caught up by the world's standards of plastic success. They create ministries in which

- Enthusiasm is more important than substance
- Style is more important than content
- Dress is more important than virtue
- And what we drive is more important than where we're going

Yet Jesus says, "For what is a man profited, if he shall gain the whole world, and lose his own soul? ... Seek ye first the kingdom of God, and his righteousness" (Matthew 16:26; 6:33 KJV).

Because the church opts to copy rather than transform society, the world's values become ours. The children imitate our actions, thus, even in church, we end up with young people who

- Own expensive tennis shoes on their feet and nothing in the head
- Can cuss on the street corner and can't answer in the classroom
- Can rap but can't pray
- Can shoot a gun and can't use a mop
- Can make a baby but can't make a bed
- Have gold chains around their necks and no sense in their heads
- Have designer jeans and degenerate morals

One reason for our laxity is that it is easier to have church members than to make disciples. Discipleship requires more time and energy, interrelatedness, interdependence, and accountability. Listen to what the apostle Paul tells us: "We then that are strong ought to bear the infirmities of the weak, and not to please ourselves. . . . Brethren, if a man be overtaken in a fault, ye which are spiritual, restore such an one. . . . And the multitude of them that believed were of one heart and of one soul: neither said any of them that ought of the things which he possessed was his own; but they had all things in common. And they continued steadfastly in the apostles' doctrine and fellowship, and in the breaking of bread, and in prayers" (Romans 15:1; Galatians 6:1; Acts 4:32; 2:42 KJV).

Christians are called to challenge

- The sleepy to wake up
- The crooked to straighten up
- The meek to speak up
- The stingy to give it up
- The despairing to look up
- The liars to 'fess up
- And the lazy to get up

ON MAKING A DIFFERENCE

As the salt of the earth, Christians ought to maintain preserving power—our presence ought to make a difference in any community.

Christians have a "gathered church" mentality that no longer makes believers feel the need to impact the neighborhood where the church is located. Church members drive in, worship, and drive back home, then complain about the way "those people" around the church live. Our churches have become fortresses in the community, valiantly fighting to keep "those people" outside.

Jesus commanded, however, Christians to "go and teach. . . . go and disciple" (Matthew 28:19–20 paraphrased). The Lord says "go," and we sit around wishing poor people, burdened in spirit, with riveted down horizons and lost hope, will come to us.

Christians passively wait for the disconnected, disaffected, dis-possessed, and despairing to attend our churches. Many times the church can be accurately pictured as people gathered to catch fish in an aquarium, all the while ignoring the ocean and rushing streams just short distances away. Thus, we end up swapping members, guarding jealously those in our care, while thousands march past our doors every day on their way to cer-tain peril.

Part of the dilemma Christians face results from the fact that unbelievers whom we ought to be seeking don't fit *our* image of the kind of material the *Lord* can use. As John R. Mott said, "The greatest hindrance to the evangelizing of the world are those within the church." Christians must come to accept, not just mentally, but in our hearts, Henry Ward Beecher's truthful saying, "The church is not a gallery for the exhibition of eminent saints, but a school for the education of imperfect ones."

If Christians headed Jesus' personnel committee, none of the original disciples would have been included in the collection. They included

- A liar named Peter
- A betrayer named Judas
- A doubter named Thomas
- A bigot named Nathaniel
- Two blowhards named James and John
- A cheater named Matthew

But Jesus chose the left-out, dropped-out, and put-out members of society. "They that are whole have no need of the physician, but they that are sick: I came not to call the righteous, but sinners to repentance" (Mark 2:17b KJV). People with prob-lems need the church, like sick people need a hospital.

If we take a look at who and what the Lord uses, we will dis-cover that none of us is perfect. We are all former liars, hyp-ocrites, pool hustlers, bar flies, gamblers, and midnight ramblers living in air-conditioned hell and wall-to-wall misery. Christians need to be reminded, "All have sinned, and come short of the glory of God" (Romans 3:23).

The Lord has entrusted his children with the responsibility to go and tell a story that is old and forever new:

- To tell a dying world, "The wages of sin is death"
- To tell somebody, "God so loved the world"
- To tell somebody, "All things work together for good"
- To tell somebody, "They that wait upon the LORD shall renew their strength"

Christians are called to be agents of change in a corrupt society. We are mandated to continually turn the world upside down for good. Our assignment is to go into the hedges and highways, broad streets and back alleys, suburbs and public housing, to teach, preach, and reach everybody we can for Christ.

SALT OF THE EARTH

And when Christians maintain our savor, when we rise in this age in the place where he has placed us, we will discover anew that the Lord has promised to be with us.

When Christians take this stand, we will discover anew the Lord's promise to be with us:

- In the sunshine and the rain
- In bright days and through dark nights
- In times of joy and times of trial
- In sickness and in health
- Up the rough side of the mountain
- Down into the valley

Jesus . . .

- Who is the "Lily of the Valley"
- Who is Alpha and Omega
- Who is Captain of the Lord's Host
- Who is a Rock in a Weary Land

Living in Hell

- Who is a Bridge Over Troubled Waters

Will be with us . . .

- 'Til the sun refuses to shine
- 'Til the moon drips away in blood

"Ye are the salt of the earth." ☩

Jesus Calls Us to Greatness
Mark 10:37

T. O'Neal Crivens, Sr. (B.A., University of Arkansas;
Memphis Theological Seminary) is pastor of the
Testament of Hope Community Baptist Church in
Memphis, Tennessee.

Jesus Calls Us to Greatness

They said to him, "Grant us that we may sit, one on Your right hand and the other on Your left, in Your glory" (MARK 10:37 NKJV).

Alfred Adler, one of the fathers of modern psychiatry, said that one of the dominant impulses every human is born with is the instinct to get ahead. Rising to the top seems to be a part of our natural equipment; there is no way to rid ourselves of this basic instinct.

Therefore, we are not surprised when the brothers James and John asked the Master if they may be his chief assistants when he becomes "King of Kings and Lord of Lords." While Jesus spoke about becoming a ruler of the new kingdom to come, James and John wanted to be Prime Minister and First Vice President. This incident reveals the brothers' self-seeking ambition and dissatisfaction with just being a citizen in Jesus' new kingdom. They wanted the highest places of prominence in his kingdom.

It is my hope this occurrence does not cause you to become disappointed with James and John. The real difference between the best and worst of men is not their instincts, but goals and ends to which they dedicate their living. The greatest saints are made of the same material as the greatest sinners.

Although desire and ambition to get ahead can ruin lives, none of us amounts to anything without these characteristics. Most of humankind's progress can be traced to a desire for greatness. This motivating drive led mankind into space exploration in spite of many obstacles; it keeps scientists in their laboratories beyond the regular eight-hour day and keeps individuals' aims lofty. Horace Mann said, "Refuse to die until you have won some victory for mankind." In the pure sense, this is ambition.

Therefore, the solution is not to destroy ambition, but to employ it for good. Ambition can be like a river running wild and destroying land. The solution would be to construct a dam to control and channel the river and to convert its raging power to beneficial uses. That is what we need to do with ambition—channel it, direct it, but not destroy it altogether.

Jesus recognized that everyone is born with the desire to excel and be successful. Jesus did not condemn, rebuke, or forbid ambition. Rather, he challenged his disciples, and all believers, to employ desire for good. Jesus urged his followers to reach for true greatness. Sin lies not in the yearning for greatness, but in the shabby and pathetic ways we often reach for it.

People tend to measure greatness in terms of power, wealth, and prominence. This is one of America's main problems. We tend to think of life as a pyramid. Most of us believe the really great people are the ones who've managed to scramble to the top of the pyramid. The higher one climbs, the more people under them, and thus the greater they are.

The people of Jesus' day were similar to individuals today. They respected and desired authority, power, and wealth. Politicians sold their integrity to Rome for a measure of power. Even the religious leaders of Jesus' day held on to warped views of greatness. So Jesus warned his followers to beware of the Scribes and the Pharisees who enjoyed prancing around in their Louis Roth robes and French Shriner sandals. The religious superiors always sought the best seats in the synagogues. They were competitive, self-seeking pyramid climbers!

In today's freewheeling age people emphasize success, prestige, and wealth. Many people work themselves into ill health, step on others, and destroy their families on the way to the top. We need to recognize and rethink what Jesus taught about true greatness. He emphasized that in the Kingdom of God, true greatness is measured in terms of service. Jesus regarded those who served as the outstanding people. Again, the solution to the problem is not to stifle ambition, but to redirect and rechannel it for good.

Jesus' call to service is an invitation to humility, and he is our example. And this service I am speaking about is not done within the four walls of what we glibly call a church. It is done in whatever station of life "wherewith" we are called.

I am reminded of a woman who called the church I presently serve to ask if service had ended. I responded, "Worship is over, but service is just about to begin."

Jesus gives specific guidelines for us to follow in order to achieve true greatness.

1. THERE IS A PRICE TO BE PAID

When James and John made their requests for places of prominence in the kingdom, Jesus asked them if they were able to drink of the cup he would drink and experience the baptism he would experience? (Mark 10:38). It is my belief that Jesus' cup of sorrow is also a metaphor for the trials and tribulations in our lives which God uses to prepare us for His ultimate good.

Jesus prayed in the garden of Gethsemane, "Father, if it be possible, let this cup pass from me: nevertheless not as I will, but as Thou wilt." Suffering is part of what God uses to equip Christians for service. If the goal of our lives as Christians is to know Jesus and become like him, ultimately we must welcome anything that enables the process.

In essence, Jesus was saying to James and John, "If you want to wear the crown, you must first bear the Cross. You cannot succeed unless you bleed." Jesus told these ambitious brothers that he intended to pay the price and would earn the right to reign. In other words, success and greatness wear price tags.

In the kingdom of God greatness begins with surrender to God's will in and through a life of service to others. Actually, service is nothing more than love in work clothes. My late, beloved father would often comment, "Too many people want Easter Sunday without the experience of Good Friday." We must be willing to pay the price if we want true greatness. God will equip us with whatever is needed in our pilgrimage toward true greatness.

2. THERE IS A PARADOX TO BE ACCEPTED

Greatness through service is an apparent contradiction to those looking for shortcuts. Jesus taught by using paradoxes. He said, "The meek shall inherit the earth." But that is not how most people think. Most people believe that the mighty shall inherit the earth—those who possess stockpiles of nuclear weapons; those who maintain massive armies; those who taunt weak neighboring countries; those who bully smaller countries who do not share the same ideology. The mighty may *inhabit* the earth, but according to Jesus, the meek shall *inherit* it!

Jesus also said, "It is more blessed to give than to receive." That is not what we normally believe to be true. Too many are not using the God-given creativity that we all possess and are looking for the easy way out. How right and how eloquently relevant was Dr. Martin Luther King, Jr., when he stated, "The ultimate measure of a man is not where he stands in moments of comfort and convenience, but where he stands in time of challenge and controversy."

There is no greater paradox than the one Jesus left with James, John, and us, in this discourse. We need to change our values. Why? Because they are so distorted that often we don't know what is important. Calvary provides a classic example. The larger world community thought Calvary amounted to the defeat of Jesus, but God and Jesus knew of the victory at Calvary. What we sometimes think is a failure may be our greatest success. People think of position and wealth as signs of greatness, but that is not necessarily the case. Money and privilege only provide additional opportunities to live up to our call to service.

3. THERE IS A PERSON TO BE IMITATED

The life of Jesus, our elder brother, provides the supreme illustration of true greatness. Jesus said, "For even the Son of Man came not to be ministered unto, but to minister, and to give his life a ransom for many."

When will we start imitating Jesus? Think of the people whom you find it most difficult to love; consider the situations in which loving is painful; reflect on organizations in which you find it most problematic to discern love; then do what love demands. What are your honest feelings about unlovely people and loveless groups? Do you ever want to give up? Does the cost to you seem too high, the demands too great? Then give prayerful consideration to the words of an ebony brother, the late Dr. Benjamin Elijah Mays: "Whatever one touches, his aim should always be to leave that which he touches better than he found it." Amen. ✟

How to Handle Leftovers:
Toward a Theology for Fragments

John 6:11 – 13

Mose Pleasure, Jr. (B.A., Dillard University; M.A.T., Harvard University; M.Div., Interdenominational Theological Center) is director of the Hope III Housing Project at the Metropolitan Baptist Church in Memphis, Tennessee.

How to Handle Leftovers: Toward a Theology for Fragments

Jesus then took the loaves, and when he had given thanks, he distributed them to those who were seated; so also the fish, as much as they wanted. And when they had eaten their fill, he told his disciples, "Gather up the fragments left over, that nothing may be lost." So they gathered them up and filled twelve baskets from the five barley loaves, left by those who had eaten (JOHN 6:11–13 RSV).

I grew up in New Orleans, whose culinary fame is built upon the exploits of homemakers forced by hard times to deal creatively with leftovers. People travel from the far corners of the world to sample the famous cuisine of New Orleans restaurants. Very few of New Orleans' tourists know the wondrous food they savor actually originated in the kitchens of common, ordinary folk. They have little or no idea that these dishes came into being as a strategy for survival of those to whom leftover fragments became presentations of great value. Who of the visitors to New Orleans can know that gumbo started out as a mixture of leftovers from the icebox? The word *gumbo* is an African-Americanism; *gumbo* is an African word for okra. Testimony to gumbo's origin is offered by the varieties of gumbo one finds in the homes of the ordinary folk of New Orleans, notwithstanding the fact that restaurants serve a more or less standardized commercial version.

Two basic versions of gumbo are found in New Orleans homes: (1) "stock-based gumbo," originally made from leftover meats, and the resulting broth or stock thickened with okra or filé (an exotic powder made from crushed dried sassafras leaves originally discovered by the Choctaw Indians); and (2) "roux-based gumbo" made by partially burning flour and fat to make a thickener roux which cradles the flavor of the ingredients, which consisted of anything still in the "icebox" following the weekend. Beyond the stock and roux bases, gumbo variations are endless: okra gumbo and filé gumbo—with or without sausage, ham, beef, chicken, fish, shrimp, oysters, crabs, crawfish or all of the above; varieties of shrimp gumbo, oyster gumbo, crab gumbo, seafood gumbo, fish gumbo, duck gumbo, chicken gumbo, and sausage gumbo. A so-called vegetable gumbo, rarely tasted outside of a New Orleans home (gumbo Z'Herbes), is a mixture of a variety of greens (a minimum of five; seven or eight is perfect), some traditional and some not-so-traditional, including pepper-grass (a pungent grass growing wild in the middle of New Orleans' wide boulevards).

But gumbo only marks an introduction to the creative leftovers in my home city. Other famous dishes include jambalaya, shrimp creole, dirty rice (containing just about anything the cook can think of), and the favorite dessert, bread pudding, made of stale bread or cake, sugar, eggs, milk, butter/margarine, and whatever fruit and sweet aromatic spices are available.

Not only did I grow up in a city which embraced leftovers as a heritage, but I grew up in a home during the Great Depression where my entire household understood the preciousness of leftovers. Very little garbage of the kind Americans now throw away ever left our kitchen. Mother found a way to incorporate every leftover morsel into another meal in one way or another. All of us cleaned our plates. Leaving food on the plate was counted as a gesture of unfriendliness toward either or both my mother and my father. The leftovers in the pot or pan already figured into the next meal. Because my mother's culinary activities tended toward the sacramental, my family treated leftovers with respect and thanksgiving.

The amazing thing to be discovered in all of this is that fragments and leftovers are precious items to fragmented and left-over people. The oppressed and the left-out seem to develop a sense of values that find divine opportunity in that which those who are in better circumstances tend to throw away and disregard. Tragically, individuals who are in a better position are also inclined to underestimate and miscalculate the survival strategies practiced by fragmented and left-over people. Some economic theorists postulate that the good observed in the midst of oppressed and downtrodden folk is the result of a purposeful and beneficent trickling down of values and a vision of the good life, made possible by persons who have it made. But gumbo did not trickle down. Gumbo trickled up! Unfortunately, there is no way to prevent this misappropriation of the genius of people at the bottom by individuals who are at the top.

The trampled people of color who are being outdistanced in the American ratrace are the source of the internationally famous dish which people now enjoy as gumbo. Gumbo, the symbol of New Orleans' international position as a source of fine cuisine, is actually a continuing symbol of God's grace and creative liberating presence in the midst of his people. Repeatedly, in the Old and New Testaments, the powerful presence of God came to tangible realization as a response to the needs of God's people. Gumbo, for African-Americans in New Orleans, is also a symbol representing their tangible faith. It is "the substance of things hoped for and the evidence of things not seen." Gumbo in our midst is one of God's curtain calls—a reality check—an opportunity for fragmented and left-out people to look back and remember to rediscover God's power through the proper care and management of leftovers. At its inception, gumbo served as modern manna for black New Orleanians. Now, every time gumbo is prepared in that city, each serving represents sacramental symbols, no matter who eats it or who serves it. Gumbo is a powerful paradigm, a potent pattern, for the care and handling of the left-over and the left-out.

In the book of John Jesus miraculously fed over five thousand people. Jesus and his twelve New Kingdom trainees visited the region of the Sea of Galilee. A great throng pursued Jesus.

The news of his presence traveled along a grapevine that was formed by everyday, ordinary folk (the ones whom the Scripture calls "the common people").

As Jesus took his seminary students—twelve less-than-kosher boys from the ghetto—up into a mountain for a review session, he looked out over the great mass of people and his Savior's heart melted with compassion for their wants and needs. The crowd left the living hell of their daily grind to seek the hope that the Carpenter of Nazareth inspired. Mark's account of this event records that Jesus' compassion was brought forth by their obvious neglect (Mark 6:34). The people appeared to be "sheep without a shepherd," aimless, without direction; fragmented, leftovers of Jewish religion, society, and politics.

If you keep a keen eye open when you read the Gospels, you will recognize that Jesus equipped unqualified, unlikely, and unfit men for kingdom service. Their role would include recruiting and enrolling new people for Christ's new domain. Jesus did not allow the disciples to occupy the sidelines while he worked. He did not perform solo when he fed the hungry crowd. Jesus *involved the disciples* in his ministry to the "lost sheep of the house of Israel." The feeding of the five thousand, the only miracle recorded by all four Gospels, is *less a miracle of emergency public assistance than it is a field work exercise in the miraculous*, conducted by the Master Teacher for the benefit of his twelve students. The miracle is a unit of instruction which proceeds in three distinct lessons: (1) the lesson of faith, (2) the lesson of discipline, and (3) the lesson of the conservation of leftovers.

1. THE LESSON OF FAITH

In the first lesson, Jesus issued a challenge to the disciples: "How are we going to provide enough bread to feed all these folk?" Or to put it in modern-day language, "Is there a bread store in the vicinity with the capacity to feed this crowd?" In the gospel of Mark the challenge is embarrassingly personal. When the disciples suggested that the people be sent away to fend for themselves, Jesus said to them, "You give them something to eat" (Mark 6:37). Jesus probably looked straight at Philip when he issued the challenge. Philip's answer to Jesus establishes him as "One of those who would like to do good unto others but who cannot for the life of them see how to go about getting it done" (William Barclay, *The Master's Men*). According to Clarence Jordan's *Cotton Patch Gospels*, Philip answers, "Even if everybody got only a taste, it would take about two hundred dollars' worth." What a situation for Philip and all the disciples! Like his schoolmates, Philip was enrolled in the school of eternity.

But also like his classmates, his imagination was earthbound, limited to the functioning of human logic and by a narrow focus on the calculation of the humanly possible. There stood Philip— at the very threshold of eternity with Jesus as host and guide— operating in Jesus' presence and the presence of that vast multitude with the puny tools of presumed human possibility!

This brings to mind Jesus' disciples in the African-American community, packed wall-to-wall in their plush cathedrals, harboring in their breasts the attitude of Philip. Church folk are not mean or people who refuse to give help to those in need. But they are simply paralyzed by their own earthbound logic and tragically limited by the short reach of their all-too-human calculations from presumptions of possibility. Christians stand in the way of God's providence in their own lives and, through them, the lives of others.

Andrew, Simon Peter's brother, did a little better than Philip. While poor Philip tried to mentally muscle his way through the problem, Andrew scoped out the crowd. Andrew went a bit further than Philip. He refused to join Philip in his "think-tank." Andrew conducted a reality check. He wanted a basis on which to *act*! Andrew's imagination told him that many people must have resource potential of some sort. His initial hunch proved correct. His follow-up research led him to existing resources within the gathering.

According to Andrew's estimate, however, he found too little, too late. Nevertheless, he transmitted what he found to Jesus. Andrew informed Jesus that a little boy's lunch was the full extent of the crowd's ability to feed itself. "There is a lad here," Andrew said, "who has five barley loaves and two fish; but what are they among so many?" To Andrew's great surprise, Jesus reached out for this measly little lunch and this lunch immediately became transparent, the means for embracing and seeing the power of God.

Andrew and the other disciples learned an instant and important lesson. The challenge of faith is never based on our abilities, powers, or skills. The test of one's beliefs is founded on *what the power of God will do in, to,* and *for* those who put their trust in him.

Again, this brings to mind Jesus' sun-burned disciples whom God has placed in the United States of America. He gave us this great land as an inheritance, a gift based on faith, not calculation. There have been gloriously incandescent moments in African-American history when the faith of black people has been rewarded with an outpouring of the treasures of heaven. There have also been dismally dark moments when the moral apathy and spiritual insensitivity of African-American people seduced them into a parallel psychic and emotional slavery-by-choice, a spiritual slavery precipitated characteristically by unprecedented sinfulness and suffering. Unfortunately, African-Americans look everywhere except inward for the scant resources we need.

God did not give to Egypt what the people of Israel needed. Nor does God give to Washington, D. C., or Nashville or Little Rock or any other seat of human power what African-American people need in this fateful hour in the United States of America! Our current paralysis by crookedness, crime, and crack is the result of being fractured by spiritual division and confusion at a time when what we need is a shared vision of God's presence and power in our midst. We need to gather up the fragments so none may be lost. The intractable problems plaguing the African-American community are directly related to our loss of *steadfast faith* that sustained our forebears through slavery, and the *innovative faith* that fashioned a productive people and a vibrant community following Emancipation.

One could say, a funny thing happened on the way to integration!

Prior to integration

- African-Americans concentrated on becoming and being a "people"
- African-Americans considered home, church and school homogeneous and parallel institutions in the black community
- African-American families, individuals and community, were far from perfect and not everyone believed in Christ, but a driving force of religious faith in God animated and like glue, held the community together

In the frenzied scramble toward integration

- African-Americans became so fixated on the details of their social absorption that they forgot the One to whom they belong
- African-Americans grabbed at better jobs, housing, and the ability to purchase hamburgers from the front door
- African-Americans lost their grip on personal identities and the institutions assuring their growth and development
- African-Americans swapped material advancement for spiritual growth and stability; gave up their birthright for a mess of pottage; lost the steadfast faith characteristic of their existence up to this present time

This first lesson Jesus taught the disciples during this fieldwork exercise in the miraculous was that in the care and handling of fragments faith is not just something nice and handy to have along on the journey—faith is preeminent and crucial. It is a necessity.

2. THE LESSON OF DISCIPLINE

The second lesson established the conditions that are necessary for Jesus to maximize what the people already possessed. God is a God of order. When Christians are summoned to experience the power and glory of the Father, Son, and Holy Ghost, we are always called to order. Moses could not lead the children of Israel from Egypt to Sinai until he put Jethro's wise counsel of organization into action. When Jesus healed the man with a withered arm, he first demanded that he stretch it forth. If the man upon his sick-bed at the Pool of Bethesda was serious about becoming well, he must take up his bed and walk. The blind man who wanted to see had to go with anointed eyes to the Pool of Siloam and wash. Before the Holy Ghost could become an anointing fire in the hearts and minds of the disciples gathered in the upper room, giving birth to God's *new world order*, they had to be "with one accord in one place." It is always thus. Discipline is required that has for us no logical bearing on what we calculate the problem to be or the solution to require.

The disciples had exhibited faith at least the size of a mustard seed. Andrew had found a lunch. The incarnate creator of all things and sovereign Savior of the world, Jesus was about to show forth his Father's power and glory. Before he continued, however, there must be order!

Jesus told his disciples, the twelve in training, "Make the people sit down." The people were 5,000 men, not counting women and children (and one child had his lunch confiscated), to take a seat on the mountain. These people lived miles away and were far from home and hearth, shelter and nutrition. They were probably hungry, tired, and hot. In a way, Jesus' command makes no sense at all. It is not logical because God's ways are not our ways. Human expectation is based on human ability, on human forms of order. Jesus must take control of the situation. As long as the people maintained jurisdiction they stayed hungry.

Obviously, the boy with the lunch came from a poor family. The bread in the lunch gave that away. Barley, which was of the lowest nutritional and economic value, was consumed by the poor. So the potential of the crowd did not yield steak and lobster, but merely the poor fare of impoverished ordinary folk. *That's all Jesus needed!* The disciples' faith, combined with a people brought to appropriate order by the application of needed discipline, is more important than the five barley loaves and two fish. When the conditions of faith and discipline were met, the Master Teacher proceeded further into the unit of instruction to his disciples.

One reads the Scripture passage without breathing at this point. "Jesus then took the loaves, and when he had given thanks, he distributed them to those who were seated, so also the fish, as much as they wanted" (John 6:11). The gift of God is sacred. So Jesus' first act is thanksgiving. This poor little fare is cherished with gratitude. Jesus took the bread and fish; after giving thanks, he broke them . . . and he broke them . . . and he broke them . . . and he broke them . . . and he broke them . . . and he broke them—until 5,000 men and the women and the children had eaten enough!

After the miracle, the disciples understood why Jesus demanded the discipline of order from them and the people. Discipline is a necessary prerequisite for man's participation in God's sacramental order.

This may provide a clue to the crucial loss of power in the African-American family, church, and community. At one time, African-American people saw God in many of the institutions and people around them—home, school, community, and church; mothers, fathers, aunts, uncles, sisters, brothers, teachers, and pastors. That is the meaning of sacramental—invisible grace made visible, something that or someone who transparently communicates God's power and presence. The Bible makes it clear that we live in a universe that speaks of spiritual realities, "The heavens declare . . .!" Jesus said, if those who followed him refused to sing out his identity and mission, then rocks would replace them as evangelical choir members (Luke 19:39–40).

When people place great faith in God, many things around them give testimony to the power and presence of an almighty God. God is everywhere! Let those who have eyes at least peep! This is the kind of faith African-Americans must renew in order to be whole again.

Discipline is a prerequisite to participation in the heavenly order. Notice how absolutely crucial discipline was in the feeding of the 5,000. There is a phrase in this Scripture passage that is normally quite hurriedly passed over. John says, "Jesus took the loaves, and when he had given thanks, he distributed them to those who were seated; so also with the fish, as much as they wanted" (v. 11). It is necessary to understand the Greek verb *ánakeiménois* ("reclining," KJV; "seated," RSV) for a proper comprehension of the passage. I have not found a significant expositor or theologian who considers it important enough to make an illuminating comment on this verse. There is an obligation to submit to discipline. Would it shock you to discover that people *standing* on the fringe of the crowd did not get fed? The disciples distributed the loaves and fish to *those who followed orders to be seated!*

No wonder there is such widespread disarray in the African-American family, a lack of power in the black church, and a shortage of positive influences in the African-American community. Too many people are standing! There is precious too little discipline! Who is calling for order? What used to be homogeneous African-American institutions are now separate and unique organizations with competing agendas, and the black church is leading the pack. There will be no recovery for African-American people until and unless *discipline is restored.*

It does not matter what the National Institutes of Health, the Centers for Disease Control, law-enforcement authorities, or courts decide to do about unsafe neighborhoods, teenage parenthood, social diseases, criminality, crookedness, public health, alcohol abuse, murder, drugs, rape, and gangs—whatever those in authority do will be quite far from the real concerns and aspirations of African-American people. The solutions that are present may very well serve as coverings and excuses, but they will never solve the problems of black folk. Only when Spirit-led, Christ-centered discipline is restored to relationships in the African-American family, church, and community will we be able to look forward to being a healed and reestablished people. Only when our churches give as much attention to the lost and left-out as they do to those who make significant contributions to an excess of "annual days," then the church will again become the agent of Christ calling the people to order—making them all to sit down.

3. THE LESSON OF THE CONSERVATION OF LEFTOVERS

The third lesson was the main point of Jesus' classroom activity on this marvelous day. One might be led to think that after feeding the 5,000 anything further proved to be anticlimactic. But what Jesus did next shaped and focused the careers of his disciples for all ages to come. If Jesus' intention had been to dazzle the crowd with the "Feeding of the Five Thousand," he could have stopped there. But Jesus was not teaching the disciples how to cater an outdoor buffet! Jesus wanted the disciples to learn how to lead men and women to salvation. Jesus desired to instruct these fragmented and unprincipled men in how to induce wholeness and integrity in shattered and left-out human beings. Jesus provided the disciples with the basic material for the development of *A Theology for Fragments*. That is why, by the time we reach the book of Acts, the disciples have learned this lesson so well that, "The Lord added to the church daily such as should be saved" (Acts 2:47).

When the meal ended, everyone had eaten plenty and the disciples felt satisfied with their master and themselves. Jesus said to them, "Gather up the fragments left over, that nothing may be lost." They gathered them up and filled twelve baskets with fragments from the five barley loaves left by those who had eaten.

Archaeologists glean the true nature of long deceased civilizations from their leavings. It turns out the basic opportunities for living life's real possibilities and potentialities are to be discovered in what the living tend to throw away. One man's garbage is another man's treasure. Jesus declares that the world's human garbage is the treasure of heaven and the compelling reason why the Word became living flesh in a dying world. In one of his many references to his mission to the left-over and the left-out, to his function as the foundation stone for *A Theology for Fragments*, Jesus says, "Verily, verily, I say unto you, I am the door of the sheep. All that ever came before me are thieves and robbers: but the sheep did not hear them. I am the door: by me if any man enter in, he shall be saved, and shall go in and out, and find pasture. The thief cometh not, but for to steal, and to kill, and to destroy: I am come that they might have life, and that they might have it more abundantly" (John 10:7b–10 KJV).

In the scramble for wealth and power, a large segment of the people cannot keep up. Super-achievers elbow the majority out of the way, and a great many drop out of the game entirely. In the highly competitive game of modern life, where super-achievers inherit the earth, the rules of the game are fudged so more and more they favor super-achievers—with little or no provision for those who have to travel from a "rearward" position. The less powerful competitors are disadvantaged and cheated for a place in life. Many become stragglers, human garbage—left behind, left over, and left out. Fragments. Jesus' kind of people! These are the ones to whom Jesus has come and they are the individuals to whom Jesus does not merely promise life, but gives to them a more abundant portion of life.

Jesus' idea of a hero is the shepherd who left ninety-nine sheep in an open pasture to search for and find one lost sheep. Some people suggest that if this Good Shepherd utilized the supply-side economic theory for distributing love and mercy to the ninety-and-nine, that same love and mercy would have trickled down to the one lost sheep—preventing the risk to person and property posed by the "unnecessary" search! But Jesus is insistent: he requires his followers to develop and deploy a working *Theology for Fragments*. The celebrated members of society must rescue, resuscitate, and remake fragments, bringing wholeness to the forgotten and seeing to it that leftovers are not left out.

Jesus spoke about shattered people in connection with the dinner that had just been served. But the banquet guests whom Jesus and the disciples fed—those "sheep without a shepherd," those lost, aimless people without direction, those fragmented leftovers of Jewish religion, society and politics—were the real subjects of Jesus' innovative "in-gathering demonstration." The lesson also highlights the disciples' role in the salvation of people. In and through the disciples, Jesus will call the captives to liberation. In those twelve men the kingdom of God was imminent! Through them Jesus will be Immanuel, meaning "God is with us!" The Savior sent by God desires for all men and women to be saved. The sovereign Savior of the world is in our midst today just as he reigned in the presence of his disciples when he fed the multitude. The battle cry of the African-American church and community must be, "None must be lost! Not one more left out!"

The disciples had learned one more time the importance of faith in their calling and the necessity of discipline in order for Jesus to work effectively with those in line for liberation. Now the Master Teacher reached the major point of this field trip. Jesus came to seek and to save the lost, the left-over, and the left-out. Now the disciples must do as Jesus did. Just as Jesus gathered them, the fragments of Jewish religion, society and politics, they must now gather up the leftovers of Jewish existence (and subsequently, the world!) for Jesus' *New Kingdom Movement*.

CONCLUSION

The church is wanting in faith. We have allowed our dependence on material things to outstrip our trust in God. Our children place their parents in a financial strain, not merely to give them shoes and clothes to wear, but to meet the pressure of their peers for expensive brand names. Our cars, houses, and associations with power are all too often the determinants of our worth.

Christians are likely to put more energy into pleasing powerful people than obliging the one almighty and everlasting God. We look more to governmental structures and political parties for salvation than to Jesus Christ and his church—the Body of Christ. We depend more on our own arrangements with people in high places for a piece of the action than on the providence of God for *a sense of heavenly inheritance*—glowing proof (in the spiritual content and context of our living) of the very presence of the power of God in us and in what God provides. We are long on religious gymnastics and histrionics, but short on aggressively creative stewardship. *We are wanting in faith.*

The church is wanting in discipline. Isaiah paints a graphically accurate picture of the current state of discipline in the African-American community, "All we like sheep have gone astray" (Isaiah 56:3). Instead of sitting down together in the solidarity of our brotherhood and sisterhood we are drifting between this or that political or religious fad of the moment, as if these trends offered tickets to different destinations in the Promised Land. Rather than looking inward and to our heritage for needed identity and strength, we allow other people to define who we are. Christians do not band together across denominations, still allowing the walls of European-based denominationalism to keep black people apart. Too many African-Americans turn to the enemy and not to Jesus.

The church is shamefully in want of an aggressive personal and collective passion for gathering up those who are victims of our throw-away society's penchant for minimizing participation by minorities. The misused and fragmented left over men and women living on the fringes of our little self-ordered existences are "sheep to the slaughter" because we abandon *them* to destruction, shamefully turning away, not wanting to be associated with fragmentary human beings because *they* drag us down. We are made to feel bad when *they* show up on the television as pitiful failures, as left-over and left-out in the wealthiest and most powerful society in human history. Some African-Americans lift their superior noses in the air and say, "We're different," "We are not like *them*!" Affluent people of color join in the periodic holiday frenzy of easing our guilt by meeting *their* holiday needs—after which *they* become invisible again. The truth is *we are in want of an aggressive personal and collective passion for gathering up those who are fragments and leftovers* in a brutally oppressive society. The disciples understood clearly the inadequacy of lip service. Gathering up leftovers is the proven strategy for eternal life.

Don't waste a moment. Make haste. As the old folks used to say, "Time's winding down!" The left-over and the left-out, all of the people who are routinely put through the shredding machine of our power-rigged existence, must be gathered up and sheltered and saved. Now! They cannot be forsaken. They must not be lost. Jesus is continuing his work and instruction in and through us—and now it is time for us to be mindful of our mortality, of the brevity of the time that is left. The conclusive importance of our limited time was established for us by the author of the book of Revelation. George Frederic Handel has framed the situation (Revelation 19:6; 11:15; 19:16) for us in the majestic "Hallelujah Chorus":

> Hallelujah! for the Lord God omnipotent reigneth.... The kingdom of this world is become the kingdom of our Lord, and of His Christ: and He shall reign for ever and ever.... King of Kings, and Lord of Lords. Hallelujah!

Now! ... Amen! ... Hallelujah! ✠

The Lazarus Dilemma: A Paradigm for the African-American Male

John 11:1–44

David L. Boyle (B.A., Bishop College; M.Div., Memphis Theological Seminary; D.Min., McCormick Theological Seminary) is pastor of the Antioch Baptist Church in Whiteville, Tennessee.

The Lazarus Dilemma: A Paradigm for the African-American Male

"Our friend Lazarus has fallen asleep, but I am going there to awaken him. . . .

"Lazarus is dead. For your sake I am glad I was not there, so that you may believe. But let us go to him. . . .

"I am the resurrection and the life. Those who believe in me, even though they die, will live, and everyone who lives and believes in me will never die. Do you believe this?" (JOHN 11:11, 14, 15 NRSV)

The Bible's account of Lazarus serves as a paradigm of human existence with hope for unlimited possibility in the present and future. I will focus on the present state of the African-American male (physical, emotional, social, psychological, educational and spiritual) through the plight of Lazarus of Bethany. Lazarus' diseased condition parallels the African-American male situation. It creates a critical consciousness for a responsible alternative to life through the Bethany community. This group of people included his sisters, the residents of Bethany, and Jesus—all embracing Lazarus through their unconditional support.

The biblical narrative (John 11:1–44), which concerns an episode in the life of Jesus and a three-member family, serves to illustrate for us spiritual and social paradigms that are particularly rooted in American society. This family consists of two sisters, Mary and Martha, and one brother, Lazarus. The geographical location for the story is in a little village in Judea called Bethany. The account opens with the sickness of Lazarus: "And now a certain man was sick, named Lazarus, of Bethany, the town of Mary and her sister Martha" (v. 1 KJV).

The entire story focuses on Lazarus' "sickness." This "sickness" creates the stage on which all characters in the narrative interact—Mary, Martha, the Bethany community, and Jesus. The "sickness" of Lazarus moves everyone to a point of active concern beyond their own interest in behalf of Lazarus. The church of today needs to be reminded that involvement beyond the selfish interests of individual members is necessary to fulfill its fundamental purposes.

Every character in the narrative, named and anonymous, centered their attention on Lazarus. His immediate family, Mary and Martha, sent a message to Jesus indicating their brother's sickness: "Therefore his sisters sent unto him, saying, Lord, Behold he whom thou lovest is sick" (v. 3).

John first highlights the "sickness" of Lazarus. The dilemma worsened as a result of Lazarus' "distance" from Jesus. "When he had heard therefore that he was sick, he abode two days still in the same place where he was. Then after that saith he unto his disciples, 'Let us go into Judea again'" (vv. 6–7).

Second, John indicates the sickness of Lazarus leads to his death. Jesus declares Lazarus dead: "Howbeit Jesus spake of his death: but they thought that he had spoken of taking a rest in sleep. Then said Jesus unto them plainly, Lazarus is dead" (vv. 13–14).

Third, John describes this sickness and death as allied forces, directing attention on the ultimate deliverance of Lazarus through Jesus' power. Jesus spoke, "And I am glad for your sakes that I was not there, to the intent ye may believe; nevertheless let us go unto him" (v. 15).

It is a well-known fact that the African-American male, like Lazarus, is suffering and dying. The American Heritage Dictionary defines "sickness" as a synonym for disease— a pathology which creates an abnormal condition in an organism or part, especially as "a consequence of infection, inherent weakness, or environmental stress, impairing normal physiological functioning." The dictionary continues to explain, "sickness" is also described as a condition or tendency of society, regarded as abnormal or harmful." John does not give details concerning the cause or circumstances surrounding Lazarus' sickness, except to make it clear he was sick and that his disease led to his death.

The definitions of "sickness" are exact, but they carry a symbolic meaning. In his ailing condition Lazarus failed to function normally with adequate energy, strength and vitality. The narrative does not indicate the cause of the illness. John's treatment of the subject made the cause of "sickness" insignificant to the power and presence of Jesus—whether its origin is environmental, psychological, physical, or social.

Lazarus' failing health affected Mary and Martha, the Bethany community, Jesus, and his disciples. We are privileged to view the sisters' efforts to get Jesus to Bethany to make Lazarus well, and we also are enabled to join the Bethany community in offering consolation to the family. They all followed Jesus to the tomb. Jesus commands his stunned and grief-stricken followers to remove the stone from the opening of the tomb. The community members help to dislodge the huge stone. Lazarus' situation presents resemblances for every human life; at some level we are all diseased. We all need the concern and involvement of others, particularly the "Blessed Community," the Body of Christ.

Looking at John's narrative in light of the African-American male, both are pronounced diseased—sick. The African-American male's "sickness" demonstrates itself in his dependence on addictive relationships and substances and his imprisonment and crime. We hear about the black male on television, in the newspapers, and in magazines. He is unskilled, irresponsible at parenting, unemployed and unemployable. The African-American male population is at risk and in an advanced state of decline. A large proportion of African-American males between the ages of fifteen and thirty-five (as noted in the media) fall victim to a "deadly disease"—like Lazarus.

In the midst of staggering statistics on the African-American male, there is hope. The story of Lazarus' resurrection from the dead profiles new possibilities, deliverance, resurrection, and faith. As with Lazarus (whose name means "God is my helper"), so also with the African-American male; deliverance is possible. In the narrative, John points out Lazarus' community of help—namely his sisters, the Bethany community, and ultimately, Jesus.

Let us examine a dimension of the story—not reflecting how Lazarus becomes sick but, rather, why his "sickness" worsened. John emphasizes the distance between Lazarus and Jesus "Therefore his sisters sent unto him, saying 'Lord, behold, he whom thou lovest is sick.' ... When he had heard therefore that he was sick, he abode two days still in the same place where he was" (vv. 3, 6). The more space and time passing between Lazarus and Jesus, the worse Lazarus' "sickness" became. Martha and Mary commented, "Then said Martha unto Jesus, 'Lord, if thou hadst been here, my brother had not died.' ... Then when Mary...saw him, she fell down at his feet, saying unto him, 'Lord, If thou hadst been here, my brother had not died'" (vv. 21, 32).

Jesus provides distance as part of the process of Lazarus' redemption and deliverance. "When Jesus heard that, he said, 'this sickness is not unto death, but for the glory of God, that the Son of God might be glorified thereby.' Now Jesus loved Martha and her sister and Lazarus. When he had heard therefore that he was sick, he abode two days still in the same place where he was" (vv. 4–6). This distance between Jesus and Lazarus leads to Lazarus' death—moving toward an opportunity for Jesus to display the power of God.

The African-American man experiences a similar type of distancing, orchestrated by the American society and culture with its discriminatory economic system, red lining of neighborhoods, oppressive government, and corrupt politics. The African-American male is psychologically and physically annihilated, blocked out of the sunlight of opportunities, aspirations, education, and hopes.

These social ills create further seclusion, denying equal privilege and opportunity. I can best describe this distancing in terms of the sunflower. This plant is positively phototrophic—it grows toward light for vital functioning for life. The sunflower grows straight and tall as long as it is exposed to light. When no light exists, for whatever reason, the sunflower is cut off from life-giving light—it droops, withers, and will ultimately die.

The abandonment of spiritual and moral values widens the distance between the African-American male and the power and presence of Jesus, resulting in the loss of a sense of godly sensitivity and consciousness. The "sickness" causes separateness from family and community—those additional relational elements necessary to his well-being. In this predicament the black man tends toward maladjusted, socially unacceptable behavior and activity; irresponsibility, escapism, violence, drugs, along with sexual exploration and exploitation, resulting in AIDS and other sexually transmitted diseases.

This distancing may be perpetuated even by the local church. When no ministries exist to address the frustrations, problems, and hurts plaguing the African-American male, he is shut out by the very institution holding the answer to his problem.

The attention from the African-American church requires consistency; intermittent caring will not do. The church caring only at Christmas is hypocritical. Christmas compassion leaves out 364 days of the year. "Holiday" concern for the African-American male often comes too late. The call of God to the Body of Christ demands proactive rather than reactive responses. The attention needs to be priortized as an ongoing aggressive operation.

The three most influential institutions in the African-American community consist of the home, church, and school.

Preventive activities must be in each place, before the distancing, disease and death occur. If the African-American male detachment is to be reduced and the "sickness" healed, it must be done by bringing him back to God through Jesus Christ.

Nelson Mandela, the African President of South Africa, presents a classic paradigm of the Lazarus Dilemma. He became distanced from family and friends and was made to be diseased through ill-treatment by an oppressive government which considered him dead for 27 years. But deliverance came through the transforming Spirit of God. Zechariah declares, "Not by might, not by power, but by my spirit says the Lord of hosts" (4:6b). DeKlerk signed the papers for Mandela's freedom, but God set him free. Deliverance for the new direction in South Africa is a twentieth-century miracle. The world witnessed a prisoner become a president of the same oppressive government that incarcerated him. This paradigm is a testimony of hope.

The Greek word for death is *thanatos*. W. E. Vines offers a theological definition of *thanatos:* "The separation of man from God. Adam 'died' on the day he disobeyed God" (see Genesis 2:17). This consistently happens to anyone distanced, separated, or alienated through disobedience to God. Much of the African-American male's problem reflects itself in Lazarus' separation from Jesus. This separation, this distancing between God and man, leads to sickness and ultimately, death.

Thanatos, death, for Lazarus is the end of a process of "sickness" that is aggravated by his distance from Jesus. The Greek word for "sickness" is *asthenia*, meaning to be weak or feeble, resulting in malfunctioning mentally, physically, socially, culturally, or spiritually—leading, ultimately, to death.

The African-American male has been and is being declared dead, literally and metaphorically. He's been pronounced dead politically, economically, educationally, domestically, socially, and physically—no aspiration, vision, or hope. He is continually cut off from sources equipped to make him a viable, productive human being. He is systematically denied access to the means vital for basic human existence.

The African-American male death notices are announced through the news media's crime, violence, and imprisonment statistics. The American workplace denies him employment and fairness on many fronts. Drugs are promoted and sponsored by the society, culture, and government of the United States. Drug addicts and dealers looking for prosperity—they are registrants for *thanatos*. Illiteracy is another organized promotion of death for the African-American male. The school systems across America do not seek to liberate the African-American male but to incarcerate him. The young male learns (from an early age, through the mirror of society, particularly from the educational system), that he is not good enough, that something is wrong with him. Read the statistics, check the numbers of black youth routinely classified and placed in special-education programs. The students do not improve and never get out of the special-education system. I'm mentioning only a few processes promoting *thanatos,* death, in the African-American male. American society seeks aggressively to put him away.

The biblical and theological understanding of death also proves relevant for the African-American male. Spiritual deadness means distance from God. Death occurs when one is unresponsive and numb, no longer alive, lacking feeling or sensitivity. A dead person does not possess the capacity to enhance or sustain life; he is no longer aggressively creative, just barren. All of these describe both Lazarus and the African-American male.

These characteristics of death are also subjective. Jesus added another sense of understanding for us when he called death "sleep." "Our friend Lazarus sleeps, but I go that I may wake him up" (v. 11b). Even in the midst of Lazarus' being treated and declared dead, Jesus did not accept his condition as terminal. John allows us to peer into the heart and mind of Jesus, helping believers to comprehend that Jesus marks death as a transition point, preparing for something better.

Death as sleep is a powerful metaphor. The modern-day Lazarus (the African-American male) is often perceived as dead, but Jesus sees him as "asleep." This indicates he's still able to experience the refreshment and renewal that Jesus brings. In the midst of the organized hostility in American society—antagonism resulting in the death of the African-American male—the African-American church must assume Jesus' attitude. It is essential for the church to say with Jesus, he "sleeps."

Because the church represents existence in two worlds—citizenship in the kingdom of humankind and citizenship in the kingdom of God—the church's view of reality calls for special vision. The proper spectacles for such eyesight remain biblical and theological. The right picture empowers the church to meet needs of the people in a holistic way. Biblical truths and principles must be fundamental to economic development, political activism, social and spiritual reform, and education. For the sake of the African-American male, the black church must rise above a singular preoccupation with heavenly interests at the expense of the diseased and dying on earth.

The amazing turning point for Lazarus came when his family labored mightily to get Jesus to Lazarus—in the midst of deadness. The presence of Jesus, combined with the power of Jesus calling Lazarus' name, caused him to come from beyond death to the "here and now" of new life. This truth provides a paradigm for the delivery of oppressed people everywhere.

Presence and name-calling (vv. 38–44) resulted in Lazarus' deliverance. What a simple but profound picture for Lazarus' deliverance. This portion of Scripture outlines a parallel posture-for-deliverance of the African-American male. Presence and the calling of one's name for the African-American male must be provided by the African-American church, declaring with Jesus, "he sleeps," insisting nothing is wrong with him that hard work and trust in Jesus cannot heal.

In my hometown, Memphis, we elected an African-American male for mayor, Dr. Willie W. Herenton, in October 1991. Mayor

Herenton grew up in an era and location where African-Americans experienced distance from almost every positive thing, with the exception of a community that loved and embraced Jesus. He also grew up in a cultural and social environment organized and planned for the "death" of African-Americans. Mayor Herenton testifies about growing up and constantly being reminded by his mother and grandmother, "Where there's a will, there's a way." The nurturing environment of his immediate family fought off all the negative pictures and forces going against this black male. His caring surroundings continued to develop his life in positive dimensions, for his good as well as for the good of others. Dr. Herenton holds the highest political position in the city. This "rags-to-riches" story illustrates the transforming power of a healthy, godly, and supportive family and community. These elements can make a positive difference.

In the narrative, Jesus did not transform Lazarus' life "outside" of his environment but rather "within" the place he lived. In the tomb where his body was decomposing and decaying, Jesus transformed his deadness into new life. Jesus does not need the "best" to work with in order to bring about a thing of beauty. Give him the fragments, broken pieces, and deadness. He alone can change them into wholeness, completion, and redemption. By his stripes we are healed, and by his blood we are delivered.

Here remains a prescription for sustaining, regaining, and reclaiming life. This was illustrated in a recent situation involving a beloved colleague, John W. Crittle, and his wife, Corine. The couple were expecting their third child, and when the time for delivery came, John organized all the necessary things for the trip and stay in the hospital. He took a blanket, quilt, and sheet in his car in the event the child came early. John lives in Holly Springs, Mississippi, about forty miles from the nearest hospital in Memphis. On the way to the hospital they ran into a cloud-burst. The profuse rain made the going slow. About midway Corine could go no farther; the delivery was at hand. John courageously and miraculously helped deliver his own son, later named Joshua, meaning "salvation."

Corine asked John upon delivery, "Are you going to cut the umbilical cord?" John responded, "No, because I do not have the proper tools to cut it. And it could result in the baby or you possibly bleeding to death. But I know as long as the baby is connected to you through the umbilical cord, you and the baby will be all right." The necessities to sustain life—oxygen, food, and water—are available through the umbilical cord. The umbilical cord kept the baby alive and well until they got to the hospital.

As long as the African-American male stays connected to Jesus through the Word—preached and lived—all he will ever need will be found in him. The deliverance of Lazarus and the African-American male is reflected in the words of a favorite gospel song of hope and aspiration:

> Because He lives I can face tomorrow,
> Because He lives, all fear is gone;
> Because I know He holds the future
> And life is worth the living—just because He lives. ✝

Bad Black Dude on the Road

Acts 8:26–39

Fred C. Lofton (B.A., Morehouse College; B.D., Morehouse School of Religion; M.S., University of Southern California; S.T.D., Emory University) is pastor of the Metropolitan Baptist Church in Memphis, Tennessee.

Bad Black Dude on the Road

And the angel of the Lord spake unto Philip, saying, Arise, and go toward the south unto the way that goeth down from Jerusalem unto Gaza, which is desert. And he arose and went: and behold, a man of Ethiopia, an eunuch of great authority under Candace queen of the Ethiopians, who had the charge of all her treasure, and had come to Jerusalem for to worship, Was returning, and sitting in his chariot read Esaias the prophet. Then the Spirit said unto Philip, Go near, and join thyself to this chariot. And Philip ran thither to him, and heard him read the prophet Esaias, and said, Understandest thou what thou readest? And he said, How can I, except some man should guide me? And he desired Philip that he would come up and sit with him. The place of the scripture which he read was this, He was led as a sheep to the slaughter; and like a lamb dumb before his shearer, so opened he not his mouth: In his humiliation his judgment was taken away: and who shall declare his generation? for his life is taken from the earth. And the eunuch answered Philip, and said, I pray thee, of whom speaketh the prophet this? of himself, or of some other man? Then Philip opened his mouth, and began at the same scripture, and preached unto him Jesus. And as they went on their way, they came unto a certain water: and the eunuch said, See, here is water; what doth hinder me to be baptized? And Philip said, If thou believest with all thine heart, thou mayest. And he answered and said, I believe that Jesus Christ is the Son of

God. And he commanded the chariot to stand still: and they went down both into the water, both Philip and the eunuch; and he baptized him. And when they were come up out of the water, the Spirit of the Lord caught away Philip, that the eunuch saw him no more: and he went on his way rejoicing (ACTS 8:26–39 KJV).

Let us look at the subject "Bad Dude on the Road." But before we begin, it is necessary, given the identity of *this* dude, to add a small but important word—"black"—a word to which all African-Americans can relate. In Acts 8 we meet a "Bad *Black* Dude on the Road!"

The dictionary defines a *dude* as someone who is fastidious in manners, dress, bearing, and skill. When I was a lad in North Carolina, we used to refer to someone highly skilled as a "bad dude." African-Americans still do this in the ghetto today; it is a great compliment when someone calls a man "a bad dude."

If you recall, the 1991 play-off between the Los Angeles Lakers and the Chicago Bulls was billed as a contest between two bad dudes, sometimes called the "M and M Boys," "Magic" Johnson and Michael Jordan. Magic was the baddest dude on the floor, and Michael was the baddest dude in the air. These were some *bad dudes*!

In the book of Acts we have another bad, black dude, a black presence from Ethiopia, from a land we call Africa today. Most of the preaching I have heard on this passage focused on Philip and he is, indeed, from one point of view, a leading character in these verses. Philip had gone to Samaria in obedience to God's command to carry the gospel to that part of the country and the uttermost parts of the earth.

But I choose to place attention on the Ethiopian, the black man receiving the good news of the gospel of Christ from Philip. Here was a man stripped of his manhood, as we African-

American men are today. Black people (particularly men) are robbed of their personhood in this country today, in the courthouse, schoolhouse, White House, even sometimes the church house.

The recent case involving officers of the law in Los Angeles, California, who brutalized a defenseless black man, merely because of his color, is only one case in point. I might add that racism is on the rise as never before. I'm sure that many reading this can give personal testimonies in this regard.

The Ethiopian experienced living in hell as a result of physical castration. But the hell was both physical and psychological. In the days of Queen Candace of Ethiopia, in whose service the Ethiopian labored, it was mandatory that a man who worked in the service of the queen submit to castration. It was, in other words, both a condition of employment and a requirement of existence. This Ethiopian, like our own black men today, had to forgo his manhood as the price for his continued existence. Here was a man who lived in hell!

Physically, he existed in hell because of his obligation to those in power. He submitted to the most dehumanizing circumstance thrust upon a human being, denial of the God-given capacity of sexual and procreative expression, forming the crown of manhood. This capacity is God's gift of sharing in his continuing creation—a gift to man and the lower animals. Above all, the male values his ability to consummate a relationship with the female. I suspect that Kunte Kinte chose the mutilation of his foot rather than castration (as punishment for running away) for this very reason.

Psychologically, the Ethiopian resided in hell because from the moment of emasculation he had to live with the fact of castration, with the state of castration—conscious, always aware that he could no longer function adequately as a male. African-American males find it hard to function adequately as males because of the hell they live in. Thomas F. Pettigrew ("A Profile of the Negro American") states, "The ubiquity of racial prejudice in the United States guarantees that virtually every Negro faces at some level the effects of discrimination, the frightening feeling of being black in what appears to be a white man's world."

America castrated black people when they brought us from Mother Africa, and we remain victimized by that crippling legacy. Many African-Americans worked jobs and never received a promotion. Others with less experience, education, and know-how stepped up the ladder of success while we stood by discouraged, disappointed, disgusted, and dismayed. When I pastored a church in Columbus, Georgia, some years ago, I became acquainted with a deacon who was in that church, an African-American man with one of the most brilliant minds I've ever come across, a true natural mathematical genius. He served as treasurer of our church for over forty years. He could not go to college because he never completed high school. This black man secured employment in the Columbus post office and worked for forty-four years. He received one promotion in all those years. A white man who entered the postal service at the same time as the deacon in my church eventually rose to become postmaster.

This reminds me of a poem Dr. Benjamin Mays, the late president of Morehouse College, often recited to us Morehouse men. He knew that as African-American men in this country we would experience discrimination, degradation, and mental and emotional castration in the days ahead.

> Fleecy locks and dark complexions
> Cannot forfeit nature's claim.
> Skin may differ, but affections
> Dwell in black and white the same.
> Were I so tall as to touch the sky
> Or to grasp the ocean with a span
> I must be measured by my soul
> For the soul is the master of the man.

Little did Dr. Mays know how this thoughtful little bit of verse sustained and supported us as we later journeyed through life as black men in a white man's world.

Now, back to the eunuch in the Bible passage. His boss, Candace, the queen, had bestowed great power and authority upon him. He maintained responsibility for her financial affairs, "in charge of all her treasure" (v. 27). The eunuch had been commissioned to journey to Jerusalem to seek further knowledge of the religion of Israel. This was truly a bad, black dude.

Some of the brothers encounter problems working with sisters in authority over them, and can't deal with it. I experience no difficulty in this kind of situation. If the sister's got more— education, ability, grace, gifts, and whatever—she's just got it. And brothers, we must learn to admit it, accept the reality, and learn to work for and with her.

The man in this narrative must have been a financial wizard, someone who knew how to hold and handle the queen's money wisely. This area hits many black people negatively. Plenty of us think we can spend money on this side of town and on the other side at the same time. We think of ourselves as what the Las Vegas casino operators call "High Rollers." But let's face it—we are *"Low Rollers"* (and some are *"No*-Rollers,") who need to put all we have in one pot, not split our money up and carry it uptown *and* downtown!

In my hometown, Memphis, an esteemed trustee (now deceased) in our church was president of a little bank worth about seventy million dollars. And even though it's one of the best-run banks in town, an employer of African-Americans, practically all of the checks written by black members of our churches are issued by the white banks in our half-black, half-white city. Can our situation get more ironic than this?

What is wrong with black people that we can't handle our own money? Explain for me this twisted love affair we have with white folks in the economic arena. Why take the fruits of our labor and give them to the affluent for the uplifting of their community and elevating of their people, while our own black communities plead for life and liberation? I pray that Almighty

God will let me live to see a reversal of this pitiable situation someday.

Back to the eunuch—the bad, black dude described in our text. Not only was this man entrusted with the treasury of the powerful queen, but on the spiritual side, he feared God. God's Word says he came to Jerusalem to worship, and on his way back to Ethiopia he sat in his chariot reading Isaiah the prophet.

This black man sought spiritual guidance, and at this point in his life the Lord intended to reward him abundantly. Scripture promises, "He who comes to God must believe that he is, and that he is a rewarder of them that diligently seek him." I've discovered if you stay with God and seek him diligently, he will reward you.

> If you seek his face early in the morning,
> God will reward you.
> If you seek him at the noon hour,
> God will reward you.
> If you seek him late at night,
> God will reward you,
> For he is a God that neither slumbers nor sleeps.

I've been seeking him for a long time, and he always made a way for me. When I went to Morehouse College in Atlanta back in the fifties, I had no father to count on, nor any Merit Scholarship, Pell Grant, financial aid, or work-study program to help me. But I had a praying mother and an almighty God on my side. In answer to my mother's prayers, Dr. Mays, the college president, opened up his heart and adopted me into his home, where I lived as his son for four years of undergraduate study and two years of graduate theological study. When I entered the college, I hardly owned a dime; but with God's help, when I left the college, I didn't owe a dime. God *will* make a way, I tell you!

It is disturbing to hear young African-American males and females complaining today because of the lack of this or that— no family, no father, no "wheels," sometimes no nothing. I hasten to remind them if they possess a creative positive attitude combined with whatever other blessings that have come their way—good health, sharp minds, strong bodies—they already hold all that they need. If a young person is endowed with one or a combination of these attributes, along with a willingness to work and succeed, and a willingness to seek and serve God, "God will surely make a way!"

Notice what the eunuch engaged in while he sat in his chariot. He read. Picture him in your mind's eye—legs crossed, body relaxed, and eyes intently fastened on a curiously compelling and intriguing passage of Scripture. "He was led as a sheep to the slaughter; and like a lamb dumb before his shearer, so opened he not his mouth: In his humiliation his judgment was taken away: and who shall declare his generation? for his life is taken from the earth" (Isaiah 53:7–9).

Imagine now his perceptive mind beginning to wonder, "Who are the sheep?" "Who's the slaughterer?" "Why? Why? Why?" These same questions continuously hound theologians, scholars, preachers, and teachers through the centuries and across the pages of time.

This is what reading God's Word will do for us. It opens up the windows of our minds so the refreshing and invigorating breezes from Heaven can enter into our parched narrow hearts, minds, and souls. Empowerment exists in reading God's Word. God says, "My word shall not come back to me void." His Holy Word will broaden your understanding, expand personal vision, and increase the depth of your love, hope, and faith. READ HIS WORD!

This fellow was no doubt reading from the Hebrew Scriptures, the Septuagint, which is the Greek version of the Old Testament—an indication that the eunuch was bilingual. This bad, black dude was a scholar as well as an economist!

Parents, help your children to develop a love of learning as young people. Expose their developing senses to great music, art, and poetry. Introduce your children to authors, composers, scientists, and artists—especially those of color. Take time away from the video movies and games. Accompany them to the planetarium, art galleries, library, museums, and the zoological and botanical gardens found in most of our cities. Life is more than Disney, Spike Lee, Robin Givens, and top rap groups, though all of these maintain their place.

The children are in our hands, malleable, makeable, vulnerable, and breakable. It is our responsibility—yours and mine—to encourage, nurture and guide them, as well as provide for their physical needs. Many mothers, grandmothers, sisters and aunts care for our children lovingly, but alone. These women need the help of bad, black dudes.

Even if you have a daughter or son on the other side of town, let them know you love them. If you do not love your own flesh and blood, you cannot claim to love the God who made you. Matthew tells us, even a sparrow shall not fall to the ground without the Father's knowledge. Men, love your sons, daughters and wives. When you love them, you show love for the Father!

On his return home from worship, somewhere between Jerusalem and Gaza, the Ethiopian was reading the book of Isaiah. Meanwhile the Holy Spirit said to Philip, "Go and join yourself to that chariot." Philip obeyed and confronted this bad, black dude with an order from on high. "Let down your chariot and let me ride. I know you're a man of prestige and power, but stop this BMW. Stop this Mercedes Benz. Stop this Lincoln Continental, this Cadillac, this Buick, this New Yorker. I've got a message that is far more powerful than you, your boss, your position, or this chariot!"

Philip asked the eunuch, "Understandest thou what thou readest?" The black man answered, "How can I, except some man should guide me?" Here, again, the intelligence of this bad, black dude is apparent. He knew he needed enlightenment and interpretation from someone wiser and more learned in the Scriptures than he. He readily admitted his ignorance in this matter. Oftentimes we read, without understanding, but something within us—stubbornness or foolish pride—keeps us from admitting our reading is not productive.

No matter how successful, prosperous, or upwardly mobile you are on the job and in society, you need somebody to interpret God's Word for you. You may be conversant with power brokers, skilled in the courtroom, adept in the halls of Congress, at home within the walls of academia, a genius in the operating room, the science lab, or the cockpit of the mighty 747—but you still need the guidance of a spirit-filled man or woman of God to help you wrestle with the life-giving, soul-sustaining, eternal, and powerful Word of God.

Then Philip "opened his mouth . . . and preached unto him Jesus." Therein is salvation for all of us. There it is! When Jesus is truly "preached unto us," and the message comes from the Holy Spirit, we whisper, shout, holler, or scream, "I BELIEVE THAT JESUS CHRIST IS THE SON OF GOD!" And this is what the eunuch did. And not only that, he commanded Philip to baptize him with water in the nearby stream. We see a new person, enlightened intellectually, but more importantly, spiritually enlightened. A profound change came over him. He can never be the same.

As you know, all stories, even those in the Bible, do not always end on a happy note. Today, in the real world, as we observe the stories on CNN, "General Hospital," the *New York Times*, *Ebony*, and *Jet*, far too many end on a tragic note. But thanks be to God, this one ends happily. This eunuch in Candace's cabinet, this bad black dude, when he came up out of the water, "went on his way rejoicing," because he'd experienced and accepted the love and mercy of God. He now held within his heart and mind a story to tell to all he met regarding God's saving power.

I wish all of us could and would go on our way rejoicing. We must truly and sincerely believe

- That Jesus is the Son of God;
- That our blackness is a blessing and not a curse;

- That the white man can't save us—we must do it our-selves;
- That our children are precious gifts from God;
- That our women want, deserve, and need our respect;
- That crack-cocaine, AIDS, pornography, teenage preg-nancy, guns, alcohol, illicit sex, and other negatives so prevalent in black communities are not going to magi-cally disappear.

If we truly and sincerely believe God is still on the throne, sitting high and looking low, then today we too can go on our way rejoicing, singing with the bad, black dude in the book of Acts:

Lord, I just come from the fountain,
I'm just from the fountain, Lord!
I've just come from the fountain,
His name so sweet!

Yes, the eunuch went on his way rejoicing. However, the eunuch's personal salvation is not the end of the story. Tradition states his evangelistic zeal became the flame God used to start a spiritual revival in Ethiopia. He became the Paul for that section of the world. It is believed he introduced the new religion to the officials of Queen Candace's court and from there it spread to other sections of Africa.

Some historians believe this man established the Coptic Church in Ethiopia, the oldest consecutive Christian community on the continent of Africa. One of our church fathers, Irenaeus, tells us (Against Heresies, iii 12:8) the eunuch became a mis-sionary upon his return to Ethiopia.[1] William LaRue Dillard also makes this point in his book *Biblical Ancestry Voyage*: "This eunuch went back to Ethiopia and gave a full report to the queen as to his mission and shared his new-found faith in Jesus Christ. I am sure he left his position as treasurer for the queen and I am sure he became a pivotal force in spreading the Christian Gospel throughout Ethiopia."[2]

This bad black dude's conversion became the spiritual thrust that was needed to bring the Gospel to another section of the world. The penetrating light of the Lord Jesus Christ was placed in the hands of a man physically castrated by men, but (this makes a huge difference) spiritually empowered by God in and through Jesus Christ. God gave this handicapped African the glorious responsibility to "Tell the Story." Truly, those handicapped by adverse circumstances are used by a merciful God to possess in "earthen vessels" the treasure of the Word of God for the whole world.

This African searcher-after-God was thrown involuntarily into hell. Nevertheless, he rose above the awfulness of his situation to become resourceful in spite of his handicap. From his example African-American males of today can learn that handicaps are not necessarily barriers to productive living—even in hell. ✢

Notes

1. "Bad Black Dude on the Road" is adapted from a sermon delivered at the Cornerstone Baptist Church in Brooklyn, New York.

2. William LaRue Dillard, *Biblical Ancestry Voyage* (Morristown, N.J.: Aaron Press, 1989), 223–24.

Uncle Tom Theology

Colossians 3:22; 4:1

Michael N. Harris (B.A., Morehouse College; M.Div., Eastern Baptist Theological Seminary; D.Min., Eastern Baptist Theological Seminary) is pastor of the Wheat Street Baptist Church in Atlanta, Georgia.

Uncle Tom Theology

Servants, obey in all things your masters according to the flesh; not with eyeservice, as men-pleasers; but in singleness of heart, fearing God: . . . Masters, give your servants that which is just and equal; knowing that ye also have a Master in heaven (COLOSSIANS 3:22; 4:1 KJV).

Centuries ago, a seasoned preacher took pen in hand to write a second time to his son in the ministry. He could sense that his earthly days approached their conclusion. He was about prepared to be a participant in that democracy we call death. In the imagery of my former colleague in the borough of Brooklyn, Dr. Gardner C. Taylor, this old preacher of centuries ago could "almost feel the mist from Jordan moisturizing his face." When a person can detect the curtains slowly descending on the stage of his life, it makes him want to put everything in order.

This describes the circumstance of Paul, once known as Saul of Tarsus, the chief persecutor of Christians who later became Paul the proclaimer of Christianity and a committed pastor.

Pastor Paul wanted Timothy, his son in the ministry, to keep some things always in mind. Two of Paul's directives come to mind: (1) "Study to show thyself approved unto God, a workman that needeth not to be ashamed, rightly dividing the word of truth" (2 Timothy 2:15); (2) "Preach the word; be instant in season, out of season; reprove, rebuke, exhort with all long-suffering and doctrine" (2 Timothy 4:2). In so many words, Paul was saying to Timothy study, learn, then preach the truth. Tell it in season! Tell it out of season! Just tell it! Because, Timothy, folks have a way of twisting and tampering with the truth to serve their own purposes.

They will try to make right wrong!
They will try to make wrong right!
They will seek to make sins acceptable!
They will assail the truth!
They will assault the truth!
If you don't study truth,
    If you don't know truth,
    And if you don't proclaim truth,
        then you will become an ally of falsehood!
Know the truth, Timothy!
Study the word, Timothy!
Rightly divide the word, Timothy!
And preach it truthfully!

As I reflect on how truth is being regularly crushed to the earth today, I am convinced that one reason for this wretched reality is that the word of God has been so misinterpreted and misunderstood, so misused that even God himself would have a hard time recognizing his own Word! Rightly has it been said that the Bible can be used to justify whatever a person wants to do. People today manipulate the Bible to justify loathsome lifestyles, oppressive politics, powerless preaching, selfish sermonizing, and other self-serving ends. I heard of a preacher using the scriptural triangle of Abraham, Sarah, and Hagar to justify his fathering a child by a woman other than his wife because of his wife's inability to give birth to a child.

If there is any group of people who ought to be champions of biblical truth, we who have been darkened by nature's sun ought to be "sho'nuff champions." African-American history reveals that certain folks twisted and mutilated the Word, in order to promote an evil ethnocentrism that has portrayed God as loving individuals on the basis of such man-made criteria as skin color, hair texture, and the like.

Numerous people have sought to put God in their "Amen Corner" and make of him an ally in their atrocious acts of oppression. They have attempted to portray God as being color conscious. They have ignorantly suggested that Noah's curse on

Canaan somehow was a curse on black people. I think about the falsity of that assertion every time the Lord blesses me, for every day I get a new blessing.

Everyday He guides my feet!
Everyday He holds my hands!
Everyday He opens doors for me!
Everyday He makes ways out of no way for me!
Everyday He is still in the blessing business for me!
Everyday with Jesus is sweeter than the day before!
If this is a curse, I'll take it anytime, yea, all the time!

Nobody can successfully package God's omnipotence, omniscience, and omnipresence into a self-serving container of stupidity. "A God who can be so manipulated is a small god" (J. B. Phillips, *Your God Is Too Small*). Yet, folk past and present continue to try.

Years ago in this country, during the infamous period of slavery, slave owners sought to present God to their slaves as a supporter of slavery. The masters even tried to suggest that God ordained slavery and God stood on the side of the slave owners. Slave owners would bring in so-called preachers to preach the acceptance of servitude and inferiority to the slaves. These preachers operated on the plantations with the slave owners in their "Amen Corner." They preached, "Servants, obey in all things your masters, according to the flesh ..."

When I first read about this perverted practice in history and then reviewed what Paul penned in Scripture, I became troubled, worried, and uneasy! I thought about how I had never heard a preacher, especially a preacher of color, use this as a sermon text.

Now, I believe in the infallibility of the Word of God. Although in these days they may sound strange, in the words of the first "Article of Faith" of our Baptist convention:

I believe that the Holy Bible was written by men divinely inspired, and is a perfect treasure of heavenly instruction; that it has God for its author, salvation for its end, and truth without any mixture of error for its matter; that it reveals the principles by which God will judge us, and therefore is, and shall remain to the end of the world, the true center of Christian union, and the supreme standard by which all human conduct, creeds, and opinions shall be tried."

In spite of that belief, however, I began to wonder if Paul, who had penned the words used by others to keep my forefathers subjugated, was essentially saying that God sanctioned the satanic system of American slavery.

- Was Paul saying it was all right for slave masters to beat their slaves?
- Was Paul saying it was all right for slave masters to sell their slaves?
- Was Paul saying it was all right for slave masters to rape their slaves?
- Was Paul saying it was all right for slave masters to kill their slaves?
- Was Paul saying it was all right for slave masters to have unrestricted and unending mastery over their fellow human beings?

In the nineteenth century, Harriet Beecher Stowe wrote a book denouncing slavery entitled *Uncle Tom's Cabin*. The pivotal character of her book was a docile black man, Uncle Tom. Her portrayal of Uncle Tom was equivalent to the then prevailing notion of the slave personality and character, and her portrayal gave substance to a long-standing stereotype of the African-American psyche. Was Paul declaring that God Almighty approved of what happened to Uncle Tom and the countless numbers of real slave men and women?

It took me a long time to come to grips with this passage. But eventually the Holy Ghost led me to look at this passage anew and to study it for the full depth of its meaning. (I have discovered that when the Holy Ghost won't let go of a person when it comes to the consideration of a Scriptural passage, it's because the text has a message for the individual to receive and to tell.)

As a black, blood-bought, born-again, name-changed, love-lifted, redeemed, and reconciled preacher-prophet of the Lord, I asked the Holy Ghost to help me handle this passage—and the Holy Ghost did just that!

The Holy Spirit helped me to see the distinct difference concerning servitude in Paul's era and the time period of American slavery (seventeenth to nineteenth centuries). In this country, slavery and the color ebony usually went hand in hand. In biblical times, however, a person became a servant or a slave for reasons other than skin color.

When economic hardship set in, causing a person to be unable to take care of himself and his family, such a person sold the right to his labor by becoming an indentured servant for a prescribed period of time. If someone committed a theft and lacked the ability required to make restitution according to the law, then he would be sold and work the debt off with his labor. The servitude of the man involved his family, as well, until his time of servitude ended.

While American slaves possessed absolutely no rights at all, slaves or servants in biblical time did maintain certain rights. For example, every Israelite, male or female, who had become a slave could be redeemed at any time. If redemption in this manner did not occur, then the servant received freedom after six years of service along with a gift of cattle and fruit. This brings to mind the American promise to emancipated black slaves of "forty acres and a mule" (a promise that never was kept).

Other provisions in Israelite law included emancipation of all slaves, whether Hebrew or non-Hebrew, and mandated every Year of Jubilee. After the passing of forty-nine years, the trumpet sounded throughout the land, signaling the onset of the fiftieth year, or the Year of Jubilee.

- During that year, there was no sowing.
- During that year, there was no reaping.
- During that year, all debts were forgiven.
- During that year, slaves were set free.

Slavery was never unending on God's agenda. Freedom would eventually rendezvous with the slave. Paul knew this, and—if I perceive him correctly—he penned his proclamations with the understanding that freedom finally came to the slave on this side of Jordan, "in due time."

Thus, when Paul declared, "Servants, obey in all things your masters according to the flesh; not with eyeservice, as men pleasers; but in singleness of heart, fearing God," he essentially said there is undoubtedly a justifiable reason for your lot in life in keeping with the debts you owe. But God, the great forgiver of debts, so arranged things that your condition is temporary. So discipline yourselves. Do what's necessary to do! Hang in there! It won't always last. Take what you must take! Serve as your requirements demand! But know, your emancipation is all arranged, in the not too distant future. This, too, shall pass.

Paul also implied, You masters, don't you forget it won't be this way always. So treat your servants fairly and justly for you've got a Master in Heaven, and he told me to tell you he sees all you do and hears all you say. "As you sow, so shall you reap."

- Underdogs today can be top dogs tomorrow.
- Top dogs today can be underdogs tomorrow.

Over twenty-five years ago Nelson Mandela was an underdog. Evil folks in South Africa thought he would rot away in obscurity in a South African prison, but when Mandela arrived in Atlanta in 1990, he was no longer in the underdog class! Mandela now serves as the first black President of South Africa. He has made the transition from underdog to top dog.

God is no respecter of persons. We're all equal in his sight. But, due to social situations, we at times experience momentary inequality in society. Therefore, "the haves and the have-nots" both exist in our society—we have an upper class and a lower class, a "Mr. Jones" (whom people try to keep up with) and an "Uncle Tom" (whom people look down upon).

Nevertheless, God knows how to uplift the lowly, upbraid the lofty, and put everybody in his place. We must know some "Uncle Tom Theology" to understand what God is doing. If theology is the study of God's *modus operandi,* then "Uncle Tom Theology" is the means by which we understand how God uses the lowly to deal with the lofty. Dr. William A. Jones, Jr., pastor of the Bethany Baptist Church of Brooklyn, New York, called it God's way of "operating from the bottom up." Paul himself suggested that

- God, who made a king out of a shepherd boy,
- God, who made a prophet out of a fruit picker,
- God, who made a general out of a farmer,
- God, who can make a somebody out of nobody,
- God can use servants to remind their masters that they are servant to "the Master of Ocean and Earth and Sky."

The omnipotent God uses the least and lowest to redeem humanity today, even individuals considered unlikely and not good enough for society.

Rosa Parks is a black woman, and it is through "Uncle Tom Theology" that we come to understand how God made her the spark that launched a major movement.

Martin Luther King, Jr., was a black man; but through "Uncle Tom Theology" we know that God spoke through him to this nation and this world.

Desmond Tutu is a black man, and through "Uncle Tom Theology" we understand that God used him to declare that one day "justice will run down like waters and righteousness like a mighty stream." South Africa may not be the Promised Land, but, by the grace of God, it is no longer what it once was.

William Holmes Borders, Sr., was a black man, and through "Uncle Tom Theology" we came to know how God allowed his assertion of "I Am Somebody," which he uttered decades ago, to be used in more recent times by Jesse Jackson, another black man, as a rallying call for a positive self-image in black youth.

Jesus, the homeless babe in Bethlehem,
Jesus, a common carpenter's kid,
Jesus, a resident of Galilee's ghetto,
Jesus, a descendant of Ruth, an African woman from Moab,
Jesus, whose hair was likened unto lamb's wool, was
God's ultimate way of displaying "Uncle Tom Theology."
He came low to lift us up.
He came from heaven to earth that we might go from earth
to heaven.

As with Jesus, our African-American heroes did not sell out to save themselves. "He was wounded for our transgressions. He was bruised for our iniquities. The chastisement of our peace was upon him."

- "And with his stripes," I am somebody.
- "With his stripes," we'll make it somehow.
- "With his stripes," I've got heaven in my view.
- "With his stripes," everything is going to be all right.
- With his stripes," "weeping may endure for a night, but joy cometh in the morning."
- "And with his stripes, we are healed!"

Like David, I, too, can "run through troops" and "leap over walls!" I tell Satan to "back off," as my Lord did.

- Back off, Satan! "The Lord is my light and my salvation, whom shall I fear?"
- Back off, Satan! "The Lord is my shield. The Lord is my buckler."
- Back off, Satan! "I'll take my way with the Lord's despised few. I've started in Jesus and I'm going through!" ✟

Part III

ESSAYS

Living in Hell: The Dilemma of African-American Survival

Hebrews 13:1–3

Mose Pleasure, Jr. (B.A., Dillard University; M.A.T., Harvard University; M.Div., Interdenominational Theological Center) is director of the Hope III Housing Project for the Metropolitan Baptist Church in Memphis, Tennessee.

Mose Pleasure, Jr.

Living in Hell: The Dilemma of African-American Survival

Let brotherly love continue. Be not forgetful to entertain strangers: for thereby some have entertained angels unawares. Remember them that are in bonds, as bound with them; and them which suffer adversity, as being yourselves also in the body (HEBREWS 13:1–3 RSV).

Keep on loving each other as brothers. Do not forget to entertain strangers, for by so doing some people have entertained angels without knowing it. Remember those in prison as if you were their fellow prisoners, and those who are mistreated as if you yourselves were suffering (HEBREWS 13:1–3 WILLIAMS).

It is interesting to note that brotherly love, according to the writer of the Epistle to the Hebrews, includes *hospitality to strangers* (some have turned out to be angels!); *remembrance of those in prison* (as though you are cell-mates!); and *remembrance of the ill-treated* (in solidarity with them, realizing the same fate can be yours at any time!). This is an excellent peg on which to hang this essay since brotherly love is the major casualty of *living in hell American-style*. In the essay I will allow significant voices to be heard, limiting myself to necessary commentary.

A LEGEND FROM ANTIQUITY

An old man and some workers he had hired were seen one day staggering through the streets of Rome, dragging by harnesses a great, rough-hewn slab of rock. Onlookers gaped and laughed at the odd sight. One of the onlookers, out of curiosity, shouted, "What are you doing, dragging that giant, ugly stone? What can you possibly do with something like that?" The procession stopped for a few moments for the men to rest, and the old man, in response to the onlooker, said, "There's an angel in that stone." Thus, legend has it, was the beginning of Michelangelo's masterpiece of sculpture—an angel liberated from a massive, ugly stone—*David*.

AUTHOR UNKNOWN

A PARABLE FROM PRESENT-DAY GHETTO REALITY

Part I

Like most of us, Miss Williams found it difficult to love all of God's children the same. Grover Junior Johnson [because his father's name was Junior Johnson, his mother named him Grover to prevent her son from becoming Junior Johnson, Jr.] was a boy that Miss Williams found particularly hard to like, much less love—and, to her point of view, for good reason. He was kind of an ugly youngster, and he just didn't seem interested in school. His eyes had that expressionless, unfocused appearance; his super-curly hair was never combed; his clothes smelled musty; the other children called him "Grubby"; and whenever he answered Miss Williams's questions in class it was always in mumbled sounds that were difficult to comprehend.

Since there was so little to really like about "Grubby" Grover Junior Johnson, whenever Miss Williams marked his papers she experienced a strange pleasure from putting X's next to his wrong answers and big red F's at the top of his papers. Perhaps Miss Williams should have known better. She had access to Grover's records, and she certainly knew more about the boy than she was ready to admit. The records, in summary, stated:

1st Grade: Grover shows promise with his work and attitude, but his situation at home is poor.

2nd Grade: Grover could do much better. His mother is seriously ill. He receives little help from home.

3rd Grade: Grover is a good boy, but too serious. He is a slow learner. His mother died this year.

4th Grade: Grover behaves well enough, but is very slow. His father shows no interest.

This parable is the story of two African-Americans dancing the morbid dance of hell that is characteristic of *Apartheid American Style*. Miss Williams's ego and pride (more the creations of the majority community than her own) have made her an unwitting agent of white America: her assignment—to make certain that the white American prophecy concerning Grover comes true. She views "Grubby" Grover Junior Johnson as *a menace—biological, economic, social, and cultural*. Grover is a child whose potential humanity is obscured by a virtually impenetrable accumulation of destructive negative life responses and reactions. His precious young life had been deposited with too little encouragement and love; poverty and neglect; and no fear of God. Without instant, specific, remedial intervention from someone who cares, he will be sentenced to a life term on the margin of existence—little help to himself and a burden to society.

Stated bluntly, Miss Williams, a *middle-class* African-American teacher, and "Grubby" Grover Junior Johnson, a product of the African-American ghetto under-class, are resident-victims of the hell fashioned for them by Caucasian America. Both are hooked on the horns of a dilemma they neither sense nor comprehend. Neither of them has the foggiest idea why the other is the enemy.

Miss Williams and "Grubby" Grover Junior Johnson provide the focus for this essay. The parable raises and illustrates some of the questions that must be asked and answered if we are to comprehend how American social, political and economic oppression are metamorphosed into the rage stalking the African-American soul and community—turning each into a living hell and leaving both sadly short on brotherly love.

AN AMERICAN DILEMMA

A dilemma is the kind of problem that a man faces when live
options, alternatives, are presented to him, any one of which
is not quite a satisfying solution to the problem that con-
fronts him. Very often when we are faced with our dilemmas,
we are not as fortunate as is indicated by the sign I saw thirty
years ago at a town in Texas called Big Sandy. My train coach
stopped across a highway; I looked out of the window and saw
a huge sign. It must have been twenty feet high and about
twenty feet square. It read: "Five Highways Meet Here. Four
Chances to Go Wrong. Ask Us."[1]

HOWARD THURMAN

The dilemma of African-America is characterized by a crisis
of personhood and a crisis of the human spirit. Only in the
United States of America is it necessary for a whole race of people
to live under an identity cloud. This phenomenon is the result of
the continuing existence of African slavery in the United States.
The sanctions of slavery have been tactfully removed from the
official language of the American system. Presidents and the
Supreme Court (a new Supreme Court, one stacked with reac-
tionary agendas during the decade of the eighties and beyond,
did all it could to undo much that had been accomplished!) pro-
longed and enacted various enhancements to the position and
standing of African-Americans. Slavery vocabulary was even considered out of fashion for a while, but as Senator James Henry
Hammond of South Carolina predicted with unerring accuracy
in 1858, slavery has never been effectively and finally abolished
in the United States.[2]

African-Americans are free and equal participants in the biological, civic, cultural, economic, political, and social enterprise
that is the United States of America at the intellectual, formal
and legal levels. At the informal "gut" level, where *white* America
gets its kicks, the brutal reality is biological, civic, cultural, economic, political and social apartheid. The impact on African-

Americans remains incalculably destructive. African-American existence in the United States equals *living in hell!*

Gunnar Myrdal, in his classic study of the culture and society of the United States, *An American Dilemma: The Negro Problem and Modern Democracy*, describes the hellish environment that white America fabricated for African–Americans in the United States. In his introduction to *An American Dilemma*, under the caption "The Negro Problem as a Moral Issue," Myrdal wrote:

> To the great majority of white Americans the Negro problem has distinctly negative connotations. It suggests something difficult to settle and equally difficult to leave alone. It is embarrassing. It makes for moral uneasiness. The very presence of the Negro in America; his fate in this country through slavery, Civil War and Reconstruction; his recent career and his present status; his accommodation; his protest and his aspiration; in fact his entire biological, historical and social existence as a participant American represent to the ordinary white man in the North as well as in the South an anomaly in the very structure of American society. *To many, this takes on the proportion of a menace—biological, economic, social, cultural, and, at times, political*. This anxiety may be mingled with a feeling of individual and collective guilt. A few see the problem as a challenge to statesmanship. To all it is trouble.
>
> These and many other mutually inconsistent attitudes are blended into none too logical a scheme which, in turn, may be quite inconsistent with the wider personal, moral, religious, and civic sentiments and ideas of the [white] Americans. Now and then, even the least sophisticated individual becomes aware of his own confusion and the contradiction in his attitudes. Occasionally he may recognize, even if only for a moment, the incongruence of his state of mind and find it so intolerable that the whole organization of his moral precepts is shaken. But most people, most of the time, suppress such threats to their moral integrity together with all the confusion, the ambiguity, and inconsistency which

lurks *in the basement* of [the white] man's soul. This, however, is rarely accomplished without mental strain. Out of the strain comes a sense of uneasiness and awkwardness which always seems attached to the Negro problem [italics mine].[3]

What Myrdal identifies as an incongruence of the state of mind, moral ambiguity, inconsistency and confusion of white America constitutes the building materials for the hell in which African-Americans find themselves confined without comprehending its nature, origin or purpose. One way toward understanding the African-American dilemma is what Myrdal identifies as the two levels of morality at which white America operates simultaneously: on one level, the high road of "government of, by and for all the people," a level of morality and rationality; on another level, a low road based on "group and racial hatred and polarization," a level of immorality and irrationality. The basis for the American dilemma is to be found in the schizophrenic psyche of white America. The clue to understanding the African-American dilemma is to be sought in the same place. In Myrdal's view:

> The American Negro problem is a problem in the heart of the [white] American. It is there that the interracial tension has its focus. It is there that the decisive struggle goes on ... at bottom our problem is the moral dilemma of the [white] American—the conflict between his moral valuations on various levels of consciousness and generality. The "American Dilemma," referred to in the title of this book, is the ever-raging conflict between, on the one hand, the valuations preserved on the general plane which we shall call the "American Creed," where the [white] American thinks, talks, and acts under the influence of high national and Christian precepts, and, on the other hand, the valuations on specific planes of individual and group living, where personal and local interests; economic, social, and sexual jealousies; considerations of community prestige and conformity; group prejudice against particular persons or types of people; and

all sorts of miscellaneous wants, impulses, and habits domi-
nate his outlook [original in italics].[4]

The findings of this highly regarded sociologist stand in
stark contrast to the fiction portrayed daily by official white
America. Like the former apartheid regime of South Africa, the
United States assumes and announces that African-Americans
live happy and satisfied with their plight. The truth is that the
Negro problem was created and is continuously aggravated, with
malice, by white America. Although the resulting tragedy visits
all Americans, only African-Americans know what real horrors
are perpetrated by the continued existence of slavery in this
reputedly free society. The fact that "The Dilemma of African-
American Survival" is a function of the moral schizophrenia of
white America is better understood when one takes into account
the nature and impact of slavery in the United States.

AFRICAN SLAVERY: ROOTS OF THE AMERICAN DILEMMA

We preach Democracy in vain while Tory and Conservative
can point to the other side of the Atlantic and say: "There are
nineteen millions of the human race free absolutely, govern-
ing themselves—the government of all, by all, for all; but
instead of being a consistent republic; it is one widespread
confederacy of free men for the enslavement of a nation of
another complexion."[5]

GEORGE THOMPSON, SPEECH, HOUSE OF COMMONS, 1851

In all social systems there must be a class to do the mean
duties, to perform the drudgery of life. That is, a class requiring but low order of intelligence and but little skill. Its requi-
sites are vigor, docility, fidelity. Such a class you must have,
or you would have no other class which leads progress,
refinement, and civilization. It constitutes the very mudsils
of society and of political government; and you might as well
attempt to build a house in the air, as to build either the one
or the other, except on the mudsils. Fortunately for the
South, she found a race adapted to that purpose to her hand.

A race inferior to herself, but imminently qualified in temper, in vigor, in docility, in capacity to stand the climate, to answer all her purposes. We use them for that purpose and call them slaves. We are old-fashioned in the South yet; it is a word discarded now by ears polite; but I will not characterize that class at the North with that term; but you have it; it is there; it is everywhere; it is eternal. The Senator from New York said yesterday that the whole world had abolished slavery. Ay, the name, but not the thing; and all the powers of the earth cannot abolish it.[6]

JAMES HENRY HAMMOND, SENATOR FROM SOUTH CAROLINA, SPEECH, U.S. SENATE, MARCH 4, 1858

In his introduction to Stanley M. Elkins's *Slavery: A Problem in American Institutional and Intellectual Life* (Grossett's Universal Library), Nathan Glazer points to the differences between slavery in the United States and slavery in other places and in other periods of history:

There exists a major problem about American slavery, one on which a reader of even the best American historians on slavery will not be enlightened: indeed, if he limits his reading to historians he will hardly know the problem exists. Why was American slavery the most awful the world has ever known? The slave was totally removed from the protection of organized society (compare the elaborate provisions for the protection of slaves in the Bible), his existence as a human being was given no recognition by any religious or secular agency, he was totally ignorant of and completely cut off from his past, and he was offered absolutely no hope for the future. His children could be sold, his marriage was not recognized, his wife could be violated or sold (there is something comic about calling the woman with whom the master permitted him to live a "wife"), and he could also be subject, without redress, to frightful barbarities—there were presumably as many sadists among slave owners, men and women, as there are in other groups. The slave could not, by law, be taught to read or write; he could not practice any religion without the permission of his master, and could never meet with his fellows, for religious or other purposes, except in the presence of a white; and finally, if a master wished to free him, every legal obstacle was used to thwart such action. This is not what slavery meant in the ancient world, in medieval and early Europe, or in Brazil and the West Indies.[7]

More important, American slavery was also awful in its effects. If we compare the present situation of the American Negro with that of, let us say Brazilian Negroes (who were slaves twenty years longer), we begin to suspect that the differences are the result of very different patterns of slavery. . . .

And if we compare American Negroes with the West Indian Negroes, we are struck by the greater self-confidence and energy of the latter—and again are forced to ask: what is it that happened to Negroes in the Southern States before 1865?[8]

Elkins bases his citation of the differences between slavery in America and enslavement other places and times on the fact that in America no formal moral and/or institutional authority existed as a buffer between master and slave, or to secure and insure the slave's rights as a legal and moral entity. Slavery was administered as a *laissez faire* socio/economic endeavor by unrestricted individuals—*laissez faire*: unfettered economic license (greed on the prowl!) used as a tool to enslave Africans as well as white-Americans. The slaveowner was an entrepreneur and considered the slave his capital investment in which he was absolutely free to exploit. At no point in the development and maintenance of American slavery did the slave achieve recognition as a person of inherent worth. If recognition of the slave's humanity (for instance the importance of keeping the slave's family intact) interfered with the slave's value as a capital investment, the owner was at liberty to ignore the slave's humanity. All of the laws, mores and folkways of the slaveocracy worked to maintain and enforce the slaveowner's status as entrepreneur/ business man. The national trend toward the preference for individual drives over institutional needs prior to the full establishment of slavery as economically viable in the cotton-producing South (and since) contributed to the wretchedness of African slavery in America.

The harshness of slavery in America, administered as a closed and repressive social and moral enclave, produced a personality type which can be fully understood only in the context of the American system of slavery. In the book *Slavery*, in chapter 3 entitled "Slavery and Personality," Elkins raises issues that shed light on the psychological impact of slavery. What is the relationship between slavery and personality? Or, to put it another way, what is the relationship between the American system of slavery and the stereotypical "character" of black people? African-Americans remember *Sambo*.

> Sambo, the typical plantation slave, was docile but irresponsible, loyal but lazy, humble but chronically given to lying and stealing; his behavior was full of infantile silliness and his talk inflated with childish exaggeration. His relationship with his master was one of utter dependence and childlike attachment: it was indeed this childlike quality that was the very key to his being. Although the merest hint of Sambo's "manhood" might fill the Southern breast with scorn, the child, "in his place," could be both exasperating and lovable.[9]

Is Sambo an accurate characterization of African slaves and their progeny in the United States of America? What is the source of this Sambo stereotype? No such stereotype associated with slaves exists in the Latin American slave system, and there is no such derogatory characterization of an entire race of people in any other system of slavery in human history. African-Americans historically took the Sambo characterization as an invention without basis. Not one serious African-American considered that the Sambo stereotype might reflect reality. The Sambo stereotype remains so repugnant that we have spent all our time distancing ourselves from him. Elkins argues, to the contrary, "Too much folk-knowledge, too much plantation literature, too much of the Negro's own lore, have gone into its making to entitle one in good conscience to condemn it as 'conspiracy.'"[10] Is Sambo really real? To reach a point of understanding the Sambo stereotype, Elkins explores the subject of "Adjustment to Absolute Power in the Concentration Camp" for comparative analysis. He hastens to point out:

> The American plantation was not even in the metaphorical sense a 'concentration camp'; nor was it even 'like' a concentration camp, to the extent that any standards comparable to those governing the camps might be imputed to any sector of American society, at any time; but it should at least be permissible to turn the thing around—to speak of the concentration camp as a special and highly perverted instance of human slavery. . . . The concentration camp was not only a perverted slave system; it was—what is less obvious but even more to the point—a perverted patriarchy.[11]

The institutions of slavery in America and in the Nazi concentration camps form a striking and chilling parallel in the one existential category they share—both were closed systems in which the oppressor exerted absolute power (with a difference to be sure, but with the same effect on those who survived!). Elkins's bases his working hypothesis on the writings of men who themselves were survivors of the Holocaust: Bruno Bettelheim, *Individual and Mass Behavior,* and Elie Cohen, *Human Behavior*. According to Bettelheim and Cohen, the same psychological profile was produced in Nazi slaves in the concentration camps as was found among American slaves on the plantation. Under the stresses of a closed and repressive regime the slaves in the concentration camps, and on the plantation, regressed to childlike behavior, like that of infancy and early youth. This transition in psychological profile developed quickly in some, more slowly in others, developing in severity as time passed.

In the process they lost contact with any outside identity they had prior to the concentration camps, developing an intense identification with the SS guards in the concentration camps, and the white master on the plantation.

The completion of the slave's settlement in the concentration camp and on the plantation came when his personality had been altered to the point of adopting as his own the values of the SS guard or the white master. He was reduced by absolute despotism "to complete and childish dependence upon their masters." The SS guard and the white master became for the slaves (both German and American) a father figure whom they identified with as weak and helpless children. The absolute power of the SS guard and the white master gave them the perverse appearance of a "father" with two conflicting sides: a cruel father who killed without fear of punishment or a gentle and caring father who could lavish kindness upon the slave under subjection to him. The closed system, whose oppressive masters used undisputed power without fear of reprisal, became a "perverse patriarchy" composed of symbolic fathers and their children.

The psychological impact of the concentration camp (and, on much the same order, the plantation) caused the basic human responses of resistance to tyranny and brutality to weaken to the point of being virtually nonexistent. The concentration camp inmates offered no meaningful expression of resistance even when they were herded to their deaths. Suicide, a decision requiring complex evaluation of the merits of living or dying, was never powerful enough as an option to override the simplicity of the need to survive. The prisoners also demonstrated no evidence of hatred for their oppressors—they loved the SS guards to their own peril and to the danger of their fellow prisoners.

Elkins establishes the case for identifying the same forces and conditions in the concentration camp and on the plantation as the genesis of a personality, a "character," of utter subjection and childlike dependence. In the case of the concentration camp inmates, their subjection and childlike dependence came to an end for the survivors. In the case of American plantation slaves, the conditions produced utter subjection and childlike dependence, persisting in a modern, hi-tech duplication of American slavery for their descendants. Being black in America is like living in hell!

Further foundation for the thesis that the psychological impact of brutal and closed systems of slavery on the enslaved is psychological regression to the state of childlike dependence is found in the study of psychology. Elkins discovers in psychology a reality basis for the *Sambo* legend and stereotype. In his *Interpersonal Theory*, Harry Stack Sullivan finds that *the estimations and expectations of others* are major determinants of personality development. These leading determinants do not hang simply on the *majority of others* in one's existence—the greatest influence is brought to bear by *significant others*, "those individuals who hold, or seem to hold, the keys to security in one's own personal situation, whatever its nature."[12]

Sullivan's "significant others" are integrated into personality by a process involving *anxiety about the attitudes of important persons in our lives*. One automatically adjusts to the attitudes of mothers, fathers, parent surrogates and other very important persons in our lives. It becomes important, from a very early age, what these significant others think about us—whether they approve or disapprove, how those closest to us estimate and appraise our behavior. These and a host of other expectations are internalized and become part of the structure of character.

Elkins hammers the point home with a test of his hypothesis, a test which describes the conditions of existence in the Nazi concentration camp:

> Consider the camp prisoner—not the one who fell by the wayside but the one who was eventually to survive; consider the ways in which he was forced to adjust to the one significant other which he now had—the SS guard, who held absolute dominion over every aspect of his life. The very shock of his introduction was perfectly designed to dramatize this fact; he was brutally maltreated ("as by a cruel father"); the

shadow of resistance would bring instant death. Daily life in the camp, with its fear and tensions, taught over and over the lesson of absolute power. It prepared the personality for a drastic shift in standards. It crushed whatever anxieties might have been drawn from prior standards; such standards had become meaningless. It focused the prisoner's attention constantly on the moods, attitudes, and standards of the only man who mattered. A truly childlike situation was thus created: utter and abject dependence on one, or on a rigidly limited few significant others...

It is no wonder that their obedience became unquestioning, that they did not revolt, that they could not "hate" their masters. Their masters' attitudes had become *internalized* as a part of their very selves; those attitudes and standards now dominated all others that they had. They had, indeed, been "changed."[13]

Those who would argue that the aspects of brutality and amorality associated with the concentration camps ruin any possibility of symmetry of comparison with African slavery either forget or do not know the process by which Africans became slaves. By the time the slave reached America he was already conditioned to be docile and dependent. The African was quite likely a person of substance and achievement in his tribal setting. He was first captured by other Africans in his inland village, then subjected to a forced march to the ocean. If the captives survived the march, they were placed in pens with other Africans of differing tribes and languages.

When the slave trader arrived and examined the slaves for fitness—those considered unfit were left on the beach to starve. Then came the horrid middle passage. Groups of Africans with mixed histories and languages were tossed together. An astronomical number of them languished and died in their accumulated filth. As many as half of them perished en route. Approximately one third of the original number of those captured in Africa survived for service as slaves in the New World. It was as an extension of this cruel sequence of capture, imprisonment, and transport that the closed system of slavery in the United States brought the process to a point of completion, effectively cutting the Africans off from their histories, their significant others, and their ways of life.

Stanley M. Elkins's thesis in *Slavery: A Problem in American Institutional and Intellectual Life* sets forth the proposition that closed systems of slavery, in the concentration camps and on the plantations, altered personalities in the direction of the expectations and ways of life of the only available significant others— the SS guard in the concentration camp and the white master on the plantation. Following Elkins, I adopt the position that Sambo is a composite of degrading, demeaning, and self-destructive human characteristics forced into the individual and corporate self-perceptions of captive Africans in and by an oppressive closed system of slavery. I also accept the belief that Sambo was fashioned out of what Gunnar Myrdal describes as the schizophrenic psychic need-structure of the white American slaveocracy. Finally, again following Elkins, I feel a compelling pull toward the conclusion that African slaves and their progeny—succeeding generations of African-Americans—have internalized Sambo and his subsequent metamorphoses into their private and corporate self-perceptions. Sambo remains an unconscious presence and force in the African-American psyche.

An astute African-American psychologist takes exception to Elkins's "Sambo" thesis. Na'im Akbar, in *Chains and Images of Psychological Slavery*, writes:

> One scholar has stated that "he who remains ignorant of history is doomed to repeat history." Certainly, *the persistence of our psychological, social and economic dependence on the former slave holders* is evidence of the validity of this adage. The intensity and brutality of the slave-making experience traumatized our social and human development. Though many writers have spoken of slavery, few scholars have addressed *the continuity of the slavery experience within our psychology* [italics mine]. The one exception is probably Stanley Elkins who developed a sociological thesis that

argued that the closed nature of North American slavery, in contrast to Latin American slavery, produced a 'Sambo' type personality in the slave.... The problem with Elkins' analysis of the Black personality, while identifying a possible outcome of slavery, he consumed his analysis into this single image [italics mine].[14]

Akbar admits to "the persistence of our psychological, social and economic dependence on the former slave holder" and "the continuity of the slavery experience within our psychology," but misses entirely their relationship to the continuing presence of the psycho-social *chains* embodied in the slave holder's creation, Sambo and his succeeding reincarnations, through which the former slave holder makes the conditions of slavery persist.

ESCAPE FROM SLAVERY: THE OVERGROUND RAILROAD

Edward Blyden, an Oxford-educated African Christian theologian, made the following observation during a visit to the United States more than a hundred years ago:

It was our lot not long ago to hear an illiterate Negro in a prayer meeting in New York entreat the deity to extend his "lily-white hands" and bless the waiting congregation. Another, with no greater amount of culture, preaching from John 3:2: "We shall be like Him," etc. He exclaimed, "Brethren, imagine a beautiful white man with blue eyes, rosy cheeks and flaxen hair, and we shall be like him."[15]

Consider now, if you will, the present-day example of a well-educated African-American. In a letter to *Essence* magazine entitled "Shame of the Middle Class," Lawrence Otis Graham, an African-American attorney in New York City and a graduate of Harvard Law School, wrote:

I overtip cabdrivers merely because they've stopped for me. I smile warmly just because a waitress hasn't seated me next to the kitchen door. I thank salespeople profusely when they don't throw my change on the counter.

My friends ask me why it takes so little to make me happy—why I am so quick to thank others for barely treating me with respect. They are misinterpreting my actions. I don't overtip because I want to. I do it because I *have* to. These acts of kindness are simply *my attempt to minimize the shame that I feel as a Black person living at a time when the public sees us as thieves, as shoplifters and as a general threat to good business.*

. . . Yes, its damning to admit this and its shallow to look at my people in such a manner, but *so long as I identify with other Blacks*, and so long as there is a Black criminal—any Black criminal—walking the streets, I will not be able to avoid feeling the guilt and shame of the Black middle class [italics mine].[16]

And the dance goes on! Poor Mr. Lawrence Otis Graham. His proud *Black American middle class existence* is threatened on two sides—he can't be Caucasian-American, and the thought of being African-American gives him heartburn. Mr. Graham's letter to *Essence* identifies him (in terms of his own internalized self-perception) as a black man whose entire existence is shaped and colored (no pun intended) by the continued existence of slavery in America! Although a world of difference exists between the unsophisticated practitioners of religion in Mr. Blyden's account and Lawrence Otis Graham's letter of lament, Mr. Graham's Sambo-sickness is neither more nor less pernicious.

As original as Mr. Graham's lament may seem, there's nothing new about it. This belly-aching by "house niggers" that *"field niggers" is goin' spoil ever'thin'"* has been a consistent and a persistent feature of "Sambo-Theater" since its inception in the American slaveocracy. The childish, self-denigrating, self-destructive, implication of himself and all African-Americans in the criminal or otherwise less than socially acceptable acts of African-American individuals with criminal and/or antisocial tendencies is not his idea—it is the idea of his white American so-called peers in particular and white American society and culture in general. Whites don't accept direct personal responsibility for the criminal or antisocial peccadilloes of other Caucasian–Americans. Why can't Mr. Graham respond to black antisocial and/or criminal behavior the same way he responds when the perpetrator is white ("We're shocked by the dark side of human nature. We admit that we just don't know what is going on with this world today.").

The answer to that question is hidden away in Mr. Graham's psyche. Like all African-Americans, Mr. Graham silently and unwittingly succumbed to a social, political and economic atmosphere, replete with powerful psychological chains, that continues in America as a closed and repressive society for black people. Unaware of the pervasiveness of this condition, like the rest of African-Americans, Mr. Graham's more than ample intelligence seeks and finds the reason for his existence in a brutally repressive society in the apparent failure of other black people to do what he's done, the way that he has done it.

But we need to be careful. We have no right to pick on Mr. Graham. He does not have an exclusive franchise on what he perceives to be his *situation in life*. Mr. Graham just happened to write a letter to all of us that expresses what all African-Americans feel in one way or another. We thank him for the letter and use a few words from it to illustrate and underline an important truth. None of us are free!

We cannot speak of Mr. Blyden's unsophisticated worshipers or *Essence*'s hi-tech Mr. Graham in isolation, in spite of the fact that they express themselves in disparate and distinctive ways. Nobody ... no one ... escapes from the harsh realities of the newer forms of America's hi-tech and brutal repression of black people: not the ignorant, well-educated, "Uncle Toms," the militantly anti-racist, and certainly not those, like Mr. Graham, and the rest us, whose psychic sensitivity cause so much personal anguish.

In Mr. Blyden's worshipers and in Mr. Graham, we have two examples of responses to the stresses of a ubiquitously brutalizing environment, with differentiation only at the level of sophistication. Each of them, like each African-American, is possessed by the Sambo demon; in need of having that Sambo demon exorcised (not mutated, as in the new and virile Sambo look-alike and substitute, the *clarencinaeum thomasiae* syndrome—a socio-psychic disturbance in black people promoting the avoidance of anything African-American not acceptable to certain segments of white America).

The African-American will find it as difficult to escape from the destructive emotional and psychological remnants of slavery (not to mention the infrastructure of slavery that is constantly renewed and maintained by white America) as it was for the slaves who escaped physical enslavement by negotiating the intricate highways and byways of the Underground Railroad.

This time, however, the only route to healing exists "overground." African-Americans must listen carefully and take it seriously when Jesus declares to the oppressed and the disinherited that the kingdom of God is not some far-off, ethereal place accessible only to spirits set free by death.

> African-Americans must listen carefully and take it seriously when Jesus sets forth that the Kingdom is at hand ... near ... within.

> African-Americans need to listen carefully and take it seriously when Jesus makes it eternally clear, however accessible and near the Kingdom may be, no one makes it there barring the way of his brother.

The time is now for finally putting an end to African slavery in the United States by staging the greatest escape ever recorded in the history of mankind.

> How? Through a massive *turning inward*:

> Turn inward by focusing on the image of God in ourselves and rediscovering who is establishing and distinguishing African-Americans as children of the most high God.

> Turn inward by *tithing* a significant portion of our individual and corporate inner strength to ourselves for our own heal-

ing and, as a consequence, the healing of our nation; with the wondrous assistance of the Holy Spirit, by *creative self-redis-tribution*—an act of love through which we make ourselves and our means available to each other.

Turning inward is individual and spiritual.

Turning inward can also be communal and institutional.

Turning inward is individual and community exercise in generating, communicating, and sharing the inner strength necessary for life toward the outside.

Turning inward is the *overground* route to a replacement point of reference.

Turning inward causes the development of a new family of significant others.

Turning inward means taking on new roles for the development and redevelopment of African-American personality.

Turning inward to ourselves, to African-American history and experience, to the hurts and needs we share makes the base of our living, loving, and achieving uniquely African-American *within* a Caucasian-dominated America that persists in its brutality.

Turning inward means action, provides direction, and serves us therapeutically.

I am not advocating a turning away from America or from our duties and responsibilities as participant citizens. It amounts to neither arrogance nor craziness on our part to hope and expect by turning inward and unleashing hitherto unknown power that we may be able to provide healing for ourselves and for Caucasian-Americans whose perverted need-structure destroys our nation.

We must exorcise the Sambo demon from the collective psyche of African America. The idea that we are a people congenitally unprepared to be free must be rooted up and torn out of American religious, social, economic, moral and political mannerisms. African-Americans must raise up a new generation of black people whose only connection with Sambo is through the study of history and psychology.

For many African-Americans this calls for a sacrificial change in the style and content of our living. We must return to the African-American institutions and human relations sustaining us. And we must redesign, in our own image, the African-American human relations that replicate us and provide the basis for authentic survival and take these precious entities seriously. I know that some of us think African-American institutions are "not about much," but when you slice through the "programs and activities" of white institutions you find the same thing, only on a larger scale—with the exception that the programs and activities *were not designed for us.*

The contention here is not that those who can successfully manage human relations in an integrated society should abandon their cross-racial and cross-cultural resources. To the contrary. What I am suggesting is that we learn to treat integration like all other minorities who successfully nurture and maintain their natural identities.

We must learn:

- How to pursue and maintain the distinctions between *integration as a primary concern* and *integration as a secondary concern.*
- How to pursue and maintain integration as a primary economic and political necessity—as the gateway to economic well-being, but involving only that amount of our psychic focus necessary for this level of survival (this is not a new strategy!).
- How to pursue and maintain our own *African-American religious, moral, social, economic and political quintessence* as *the* primary necessity—relegating integration not necessary to our moral, social, economic, and political survival to secondary, even third, status.

We must evolve a way of making it in America *as African-Americans* without living in hell while doing so! It may turn out that the only strategy available to African-Americans for achieving this goal, as long as conditions inimical to equitable minority survival exist, is deliberate and meticulous existence in two worlds at the same time!

Black people must return to African-American institutions, even if the leadership potions that are offered to us are not what we think we ought to have. We must learn to "be there" and learn that our "being there" is really the gift we have to offer. In quiet, non-confrontational ways we must give our African-American institutions and our African-American human relations assistance in rethinking, redefining and redeveloping themselves. Both of them must be built up, amplified, and rendered capable of offering the full range of nurture, support and guidance that African-Americans need, especially our youth. African-American establishments and relations must become the signboards in the African-American community that read: MANY PATHS CONVERGE HERE. MANY WAYS TO GO WRONG. ASK US.

Turning inward cannot happen automatically, nor can it be left as a function of isolated individual action. Local and national agendas and strategies are essential and need to be developed. To many individuals and communities, turning inward will be, in large part, a private and personal experience for the African-American community (the time will come when the result of the experience will be healing for the nation as well).

Although such a process cannot be accomplished in secret, we must avoid the now ubiquitous news conference and the notoriety of glaring public exposure. Turning inward can and should be done quietly ... privately ... *within* the African-American community. Such a strategy should not come from one component of the African-American constituency. Groups of leaders and thinkers; ordinary, everyday brothers and sisters should be brought together in every city and town to think through the implications of such an undertaking—including the structure, content, and program that will be necessary.

The process of turning inward must not become *another* organization and it must be achieved through all the existing modalities of African-American brotherhood and sisterhood. Every relationship or shred of relationship already existent in the African-American community must be utilized, with openness to newly evolving relationships that are becoming the equipment for twenty-first century African-Americans. This means no segment of the African-American community can be left out in the planning that is done on the front end. It will not be easy. In fact, it will probably get quite messy before the clouds dissipate and the path to healing is cleared. In the process, however, there will be pleasant discoveries of strengths, talent and genius—some individual and community resources that have never been tapped.

The process of turning inward will have to be bottom-upwards, with the agenda set by those normally saying little or nothing in the church and the community—the ones left out of decision-making—and with the more powerful church and community decision-makers serving as facilitators, as those whose education, expertise, and connections make the agenda set by the "formerly cast off" become living reality.

Funding for the process should not be a consideration. African-Americans are capable of raising all of the money we need to do what we really want to do.

The tithe of focus, attention, energy, and resources will be dedicated to the re-establishment and maintenance of African-American brotherhood and sisterhood. But brotherhood/sisterhood involves more than just the words. So, when the good Lord grants you the very special opportunity of entertaining a stranger, you must take her/him under your wings and nurture, lead and guide her/him—you must become and be a "significant other" in and to the constituency of the African-American community. By so doing you will be safeguarding brotherly/sisterly love in continuity; you will be showing hospitality to strangers and discovering that *many* are angels; you will be remembering those who are in prison as though you are their cellmates; and you will be remembering the ill-treated with an intense feeling of solidarity because you are vulnerable to the same victimization.

It must be added that in the process of re-establishing and maintaining African-American brotherhood/sisterhood, we must not accept the assistance of supportive groups and institutions whose alliance with us comes at the price of their input in determining who and what make up the African-American constituency.

Do you remember Miss Williams and "Grubby" Grover Junior Johnson—two people who are living in a hell that is not of their design and of which they are not conscious? Well, the good Lord gave both of them a special opportunity and they took advantage of the gift. Each of them turned inward, achieved personal renewal in a new and creatively powerful "significant other," and established a brother/sister relationship for now and for eternity.

A PARABLE FROM PRESENT-DAY GHETTO REALITY

Part II

Christmas came that year and the boys and girls of Miss Williams' fifth-grade class brought her Christmas presents. They piled their presents high on her desk and crowded around to watch her open them. Much to Miss Williams' surprise, there was one from "Grubby" Grover Junior Johnson. It was characteristically ugly—wrapped in brown paper held together with plastic tape, with a message on it that read simply: "For Miss Williams from Grover."

When she opened Grover's gift, out fell a gaudy rhinestone bracelet and a bottle of cheap perfume. The other boys and girls began to giggle over "Grubby's" gifts, but Miss Williams had at least enough grace to silence them immediately, putting the bracelet on and some of the perfume on her wrist. Holding her wrist up for the others, she said: "Doesn't it smell lovely?" and the children, taking the cue from their teacher, readily agreed with "oohs" and "aahs."

At the end of the day, when school was over and the other children were gone, Grover Junior Johnson lingered behind. Slowly, he came over to the desk and said softly, "Miss Williams ... Miss Williams ... you smell just like my mother ... and her bracelet looks real pretty on you, too. I'm glad... you like my presents."

When "Grubby" left, Miss Williams got down on her knees and asked God to forgive her. The next day, the children in Room 111 were greeted by a new teacher. Something had happened to her. Miss Williams had become a different person, committed to loving her children with a passion not known before, especially the slow ones. Especially Grover Junior Johnson! By the end of that year, Grover showed dramatic improvement. He had caught up with many of the students and was even ahead of some.

The years went by, and Miss Williams lost touch with the fifth-graders of that class, until one day she found a note in her mailbox. It read, simply: "Dear Miss Williams, I wanted you to be the first to know. I will be graduating second in my class from high school. Love, Grover Junior Johnson."

Four years later, another note came: "Dear Miss Williams, they just told me I will be graduating first in my class. I wanted you to be the first to know, because you did so much for me and I am so grateful. The university has not been easy, but I've loved it."

And four years later, again: "Dear Miss Williams, as of today, I am Grover Junior Johnson, M.D. How about that? I wanted you to be the first to know. I am getting married next month, the 27th to be exact, and I was wondering if you would come and sit where my mother would sit if she were alive? You are the only family I have now. Dad died last year. Hopefully, and with love, Grover Junior Johnson."

I'm told that Miss Williams went to that wedding and sat where Grover's mother would have sat. She earned the right to sit there, for beneath the stony, glazed-over surface of a life even she'd found hard to like, *she'd heard the sound of muffled wings and helped to set an angel free.*[17] ✞

Notes

1. Howard Thurman, *Temptations of Jesus* (Richmond, Ind.: Friends United Press, 1978), 23.

2. Cf. Hosea Easton, *A Treatise on the Intellectual Character, and Civil and Political Condition of the Colored People of the United States; and the Prejudice Exercised Towards Them* (Boston: 1837); Gilbert Osofsky, *The Burden of Race: A Documentary History of Negro-White Relations in America* (New York: Harper & Row, 1967), 66f.

It is a remarkable fact that the moment the colored people show signs of life—any indication of being possessed with redeeming principles, that moment an unrelenting hatred arises in the mind which is inhabited by that foul fiend, prejudice; and the possessor of it will never be satisfied, until those indications are destroyed; space, time, nor circumstance, is no barrier to its exercise. . . . Let the oppressed assume the character of capable men in business, either mercantile, mechanical, or agricultural—let them assume the right of exercising themselves in the use of the common privileges of the country—let them claim the right of enjoying liberty, in the general acceptation of that term—let them exercise the right of speech and thought—let them presume to enjoy the privileges of the sanctuary and the Bible—let their souls be filled with glory of God, and wish to bow the knee at the sacred altar, and commemorate the dying love of Christ the Lord—let them seek a decent burial for their departed in the church yard—and they are immediately made to feel that they are as a carcass destined to be preyed upon by the eagles of persecution. Thus they are followed from life's dawn to death's doom.

Cf. also, Jennifer L. Hochschild, *The New American Dilemma: Liberal Democracy and School Desegregation* (New Haven: Yale University Press, 1984), 5.

Some argue that racism is not simply an excrescence on a fundamentally healthy liberal democratic body but is part of what shapes and energizes the body. In this view, liberal democracy and racism in the United States are historically, even inherently, reinforcing; American society as we know it exists only because of its foundation in racially based slavery, and it thrives only because racial discrimination continues. The apparent anomaly is an actual symbiosis.

3. Gunnar Myrdal, *An American Dilemma: The Negro Problem and Modern Democracy* (New York: Harper & Row, 1962), lxix.

4. Ibid., lxxi.

5. Burton Stevenson, comp., *The Home Book of Quotations*, 10th ed. (New York: Dodd, Mead, 1967), 1842.

6. *Congressional Globe*. 46 vols. Washington, D.C.: 1834–73.

7. Nathan Glazer, "Introduction" to *Slavery: A Problem in American Institutional and Intellectual Life*, by Stanley M. Elkins (New York: Grossett's Universal Library, 1963), ix.

8. Ibid., x.

9. Stanley M. Elkins, *Slavery: A Problem in American Institutional and Intellectual Life*, 3d ed. (Chicago: University of Chicago Press, 1976), 82.

10. Ibid., 84.

11. Ibid., 104.

12. Ibid., 119f.

13. Ibid., 122f.

14. Na'im Akbar, *Chains and Images of Psychological Slavery* (Jersey City: New Mind Productions, 1984), 32f.

15. Akbar, *Psychological Slavery*, 46.

16. Lawrence Otis Graham, "Shame of the Middle Class," *Essence*, April 1991.

17. Author unknown; the story has been retold by various writers, including Tony Campolo, *Who Switched the Price Tags?* (Waco, Tex.: Word Books, 1987).

The Conquest of Hell: An Essay

Charles William Butler (B.A., Philander Smith College; B.D., Union Theological Seminary; M.Div., Union Theological Seminary) is pastor of the New Calvary Baptist Church in Detroit, Michigan.

The Conquest of Hell: An Essay

Let the reader define *hell,* and I feel confident that by that definition, the life of African-Americans—especially African-American males—has been a life of hell.

Advent with a capital "A" is defined to mean the appearance or the arrival of a very special or notable person. When the word is capitalized in Christian usage it refers specifically to the birth of Jesus. When it is used without the "a" capitalized, it can mean the appearance or arrival of any person at any place or time. Whether *advent* is understood as being capitalized or not, everything and every being that appears in time has taken the first step toward an exit from time. This is based on the biblical claim that heaven and earth will pass away. Therefore, we can declare, based on that assertion and our experience, every *advent* begins an *exodus.* In fact, the goal of *advent* is *exodus.* Every being enters time on a journey out of time. Our entrance becomes the first step toward our exit.

It seems appropriate, therefore, to talk about the condition of African-Americans in general and American black males in particular, against the back-drop of this biblical event called Exodus for these reasons: (1) The Exodus account portrayed as God's involvement in the liberation of his people from the hell of enforced domination and exploitation; (2) the Exodus account reflects the Divine role and process in guiding his dominated and exploited people to a new and glorious *advent*; and (3) the Exodus account lifts into clear view the agonizing struggle of re-educating the people for a life of advent—for the burden of freedom and for the struggle involved in giving birth to a people capable of understanding, accepting, and implementing this novel role called nationhood, or peoplehood, if it is a people with-in a nation. In a most basic sense, life can be viewed as a series of microcosmic cycles of *advent* and *exodus* replicating the biblical account.

The Exodus experience proves that conquest of a life of hell is not achieved by the physical relocation of a people. If this were the case, Israel would have been home free after its escape from Goshen, and blacks would have been home free, also, after their migration to the "freedom" up north. Critical to the escape from hell remains the mental and spiritual *exodus*. The conviction firmly stating "I am" and "I can." It also says, "I must define me," because the definition of my identity determines both my confidence in myself and my ability to perform. The goal of every *advent* is still *exodus*.

THE BASIS AND REALITY OF HELL

The common understanding of hell is derived from the apocalyptic views of ancient religious literature, including the Bible. These early documents portrayed hell as that place where justice will be exacted of humans who lived on earth and did not reach a *specified moral level required by a religious discipline.* Or hell means a place of eternal tortures in the afterlife from whence self-surrender to divinity and the resultant self-control exercised by humans could combine enough good deeds with divine grace to escape. Hell, in these gems of religious literature was seen as the equalizer and just reward of those who took advantage of and enjoyed earth's pleasures without effort to relieve the misery of others or the reasonable reward of those seeking to profit from inflicting injustice on others. Most frequently, hell was believed to be a permanent state beyond time or history guaranteed a form of moral equity. Though the pain inflicted by the perpetrator that "sent" him to hell is often painted through the eyes of the sufferer, there seems to be little expectation that *the hell suffered here and now* by the oppressed victim will be relieved. There appears to be a helplessness that the hell of victimization in history could ever be redressed in history. Thus, the hope and need of heaven and hell are necessary for human sanity and human survival.

The view of hell as a condition totally beyond history reflects also the hopelessness of those who suffered injustice in history. So powerful were their oppressors that God alone, in another aeon, could requires redress. Man's free will, accorded by God, seems to have shackled the power of God to make immediate redress. Add to this concept one other, that what happens in time is the will of God, permissively or otherwise, and one begins to understand the acquiescence of the oppressed.

The great religions of the world, notably Christianity, are not totally agreed that the victim must be blamed for her/his being victimized. They tend to pose the question: "If hell in this life is the appropriate reward for those who oppress the unreservedly weak in history, then how does one understand the hell of *undeserved* and *unwarranted* suffering unjustly inflicted on the oppressed in history?" Should such sufferers accept it as redemptive and be grateful for their part in a redemptive plan? Do they conclude with Job it is beyond human understanding? Do they acquiesce under the galling yoke of unjust afflictions? Or is there a role and a remedy for the oppressiveness of historical hells?

Before we attempt to address the various forms in which this question arises, it seems appropriate to define more specifically what appears to be the cause of historical hell.

HISTORICAL HELL

Is there a simple definition of historical hell as distinguished from supra-historical hell? Can we anchor such a definition in biblical thought? Or is hell only a supra-historical state where all rectification of injustices are delayed by the super-sovereign and one is condemned to "grin and bear it" while we "wait for God" to act with ultimate judgment beyond life on earth.

Nothing is clearer in biblical records then this truth that the God of the Bible is also the God of history. The God in history who made history and made it the arena of his action on our behalf.

The account of creation with which the Bible opens is the definitive declaration that God is God precisely because he is God in the arena of human affairs—in history.

- As creator, he is God over time.
- As providential deliverer, he is God in time.
- As Judge, he is God beyond time.
- It is in his arenas over history and in history we are challenged to *understand* and to *act*. It is *in* the historical arena we are introduced to hell and the recurring drama perpetuating hell in human affairs.

HELL IS HISTORY DISTORTED BY HUMANS

Hell appears and remains when and where humanity rejects the Creator's diversity.

The creation is a symphony of diversity in both plants and animals. God certainly loves diversity. He made so many different beings and things. His disdain of duplication constrained him to display his inexhaustible creativity by making plants of the same species unique. In his creation no absolute replicas exist! And his great respect for uniqueness led him to exclaim after each creative act, "It is good!"—without qualifications.

Nothing was half good or three quarters good. On everything he made one stamp, "Good." Black man—good. Red man—good. Yellow man—good. White man—good. All with the same rating. None of the individuals in God's universe received a "superior," "fair" or "poor" rating, all are labeled "Good!"

Life in hell begins when humanity rejects as "not good," or "not good as," any part of God's created diversity. Such rejection is the fundamental presupposition of all prejudice. It is rooted in the inherent insecurity of those who find such attitudes acceptable and necessary to sustain their self-esteem. Rejection of created diversity is the best barometer of one's own social self-acceptance and sense of worth. To declare by word or deed any segment of God's diverse creation is inferior illustrates both defiance of God and the need to assure one's own worth by depreciating the worth of others. It is the seed and substance for rejection of the diverse and the arrogance required to assure the inadequate individuals they posses worth. The rejection of created diversity is the first step on the low-way to hell.

So, hell begins as human *self-assessment* that either creates a hellish condition or allows such a hellish condition to be accepted by those upon whom it is thrust.

THE RESPONSE TO HELL ON EARTH

The *advent* of hell requires the answer of *exodus* as the sole valid response of humanity "living in hell" on earth. The Bible clearly *accepts the reality of* historical hell, but the Bible firmly *rejects submission to* historical hell as God's will. The Torah, the history, the prophets, the whole New Testament story of Jesus and the Church—all represent processes that deny one the option of submitting to historical hell or the right to create it. Exodus, as portrayed biblically, follows a systematic course to liberation from such hell.

Since hell is pictured everywhere as defiance of the Creator's will and the created order, successful resistance to hell demands compliance with the Creator's will and confluence with the created order. Acceptance of hell is a loss of proper perspective and a distortion or destruction of will. That is why any successful response to hell is impossible without the following steps:

1. *Admission that hell is real and one is in hell*—not on the way to hell—as long as society condones the belief that diversity permits dividing up people into social classes and stratification allows one to believe the "different" ones are less acceptable.

Recognition that the obvious rejection of Divine diversity creates a temporal hell is step one in the right direction.

2. *Recognition of the reality of hell* on earth should stimulate the proper desire to avert it, escape it and/or prevent it's impact if not its continuity. Recognition that one is viewed as a negative entity. The first requirement for stimulation to response since the condition of hell has anesthetic power over its victims. Such mental and emotional anesthesia leaves one believing the condition is the norm, is deserved and not to be resisted. Recognition has not been effective until the sensitivity level is raised to a point of unrelenting desire to resist this condition.

3. *Desire* is empty unless it is translated into *will*. To *want* can remain cognitive only and never move to the point of action. *Will* is used to express a compelling demand for reaction. In this case it would be persistent reaction to the state and condition of hell, founded on the conviction that hell is a damaging distortion of reality as God made it and intends it to be.

4. When one wills to escape hell, one must *plan* and prepare for this *exodus*. No preparation is more critical than the mental-emotional readiness in this equation. The fundamental plan is one that "converts" the negative attitude and brainwashing leading the oppressed to believe the assessment made of them by others is both correct and deserved. (Believing this, the oppressed become vehicles to continue this self-delusion!). It is a whole process of re-education. Not until this "internal" conversion is effected can there be any hope that an effective plan to overthrow and/or convert hell will be successfully implemented. No part of the flight from hell is more important than this phase. It will require the best of all our resources!

5. The implementation of the process of escape is next and demands the power of a leader capable of instilling faith in the followers, preparing a foundation for successor leadership, creating a "story," myth and/or rules that are sacramentalized to give permanence to the process.

The process of escape must be empowered with external resources also. (The Israelites were ordered to take all their belongings and to take a reparation payment as well—the gold, silver and jewels of their oppressors.)

6. Finally, the process of escape must be transformed into a history and tradition told and retold. This rehearsal of the history and tradition of escape reinforces the *will* to remain vigilant and prepared to prevent a slipping back into hell! This is best done in the context of religious ritual and teaching.

It seems clear that the origin of historical hell is found in human rejection of Divine diversity. The book of Exodus is an external response to the historical hell of oppression in all forms. It sets in clear focus the "players," their roles, the plan and process, the goal and the price of remaining liberated from hell. Our function is to apply this classical and operational technique to our own problems by discovering the common denominator unifying us in this purpose and applying the proven process of breaking out of hell! ✛

Afterword

Board a Cosmos Explorer space vessel with me, and we will travel backward in time at "warp speed." When we arrive at the space-time coordinates for our journey, we are in Babylon, Babylonia. The year is 539 B.C. Great Babylonia's career as a major world power has hung in the balance for some time now. All is in disarray. God's judgment upon Babylonia is about to be meted out. Cyrus the Persian presently at the gates—accompanied by a monstrous war machine that sweeps nations from the face of the earth on one hand and frees Jews from their Babylonian captivity, returning them to the Promised Land, on the other. Everyone is scrambling for a way out, for a safe lane away from the path of forthcoming death and destruction. Isaiah, a witness in more than one sense, describes the scene of impending catastrophe with scathingly derisive irony, "The idols of Babylon, Bel and Nebo, are being hauled away on ox carts! But look! The beasts are stumbling! The cart is turning over! The gods are falling out onto the ground! Is that the best that they can do? If they cannot even save themselves from such a fall, how can they save their worshipers from Cyrus?" (Isaiah 46:1–2 LB).

Isaiah's keen powers of observation extended well beyond the obvious. He was a charter member of the Diaspora-in-captivity when judgment arrived at Babylonia. It is interesting to imagine how someone other than an Isaiah might have responded to those explosive events with the assistance of state-of-the-art contrivances from our high-tech era.

Someone from our era, for instance a radio, newspaper or television reporter, busy gathering responses from the man and woman on the street, and "news bytes" from the numerous news conferences called by government officials who (on their way out town) want to put positive spins on their personal contributions to the current situation. Experts on various (un)related subjects brought together in hastily organized TV forums to point the finger of blame at each other, this or that person, group, institution or development. Administrative officials called to account for not achieving a diplomatic settlement in Babylo-Persian relations. Recriminations against the military would be high-pitched and heated. The private sector blaming the public sector, and vice-versa. Some focus on institutional failure—on the inability of the government, the society, the culture, the educational establishment, and the family to provide for the order, stability and safety of the populace under emerging difficult circumstances. Others suggest question whether the system of education adequately supported to render it capable of meeting the requirements of a fast-changing international situation. Liberals, conservatives and all other shades of opinion and persuasion which would each in their turn make plain that which averted the now-certain tragedy. There would be a steady stream-of-consciousness iteration of opinions without a necessary interposition of established fact or certified truth. But established fact and certified truth were Isaiah's mainstays. Isaiah looked beyond the obvious and the temporal. God showed him the hidden and the eternal.

What Isaiah saw was not something suddenly coming into being on the day Cyrus' troops began storming the gates of Babylon City. The root of the rot in Babylonia, the source of failure, is revealed in what Babylonians trusted; looked to for security and comfort; and vested with ultimate value. That Babylonia's gods were idols, inanimate things without power to save or destroy, is the telling point. Of even greater significance remains the fact Babylonia's gods were *home-made* and *hand-made*—manufactured in Babylonia, by Babylonians, and for Babylonians—gods under whom the enslavement of Jews was proper and appropriate because slavery afforded an efficient utilization of free labor. I do not think that it would have mattered much if Jehovah had been Babylon's God. Babylon's values, Babylon's source of national pride and international identity, would still have been consistent with devotion to *home-made* and *hand-made* gods.

Only subsequent reflection by unbiased scholars can properly estimate the actual cost to America of her *home-made* and *hand-made* gods—the great god Greed and a train of lesser gods (born of innate notions of subaltern status in the generality of whites), who sponsor the social, political and economic mechanism that effectuates and maintains African-American inferiority and second-class existence (the existential equivalent of hell); and who render the nation unable to fully utilize the enormous amount of genius and good that God has made available in and through black people. There can be no doubt the cost in unrealized human potential, compounded by the ravages of rage, crime and welfare, is staggering and still climbing! Slavery might have been an efficient utilization of free manpower at the expense of captive Africans (if, along with recipient of the 1993 Nobel Prize in Economics, one discounts morality!), but the continued enforcement of a slave regime upon freed Africans has been wasteful and crippling, not to mention un-Godly, immoral, unconstitutional, and, from time to time, illegal.

Under such conditions—when the moment of certified truth arrives and during the period of time when judgment is being meted out—a nation which operates under the aegis of *home-made* and *hand-made* gods experiences cosmic and terrestrial embarrassment. These *home-made* and *hand-made* gods are the stylistic representations of human desire and speculation—they have no power and cannot save their worshipers. More spectacularly, they cannot even save themselves! What had heretofore provided a basis for the claim to superpower status begins to erode, to evaporate. The nation begins to decline, in her own eyes and in the eyes of others. Hitherto lesser nations exploit advantages that have been squandered—to the lesser nations—benefit! To the satisfied amusement of an onlooker like Isaiah, the gods made with hands are spilled out onto the ground in the greedy scramble for cover and recovery. The prophet's description of events records the moment (to use the title of a Jack London short story) "When God Laughed." When God laughs neither the provocation nor his response is funny. This is the stuff of unnecessary and unwelcome tragedy.

MOSE PLEASURE, JR., SECRETARY
THE MELAS EKKLESIA GROUP